GOD'S RESOLVE TO Create

NEW HEAVENS and NEW EARTH

LESLIE EARWOOD

WESTBOW
PRESS®
A DIVISION OF THOMAS NELSON
& ZONDERVAN

WestBow Press books may be ordered through booksellers or by contacting:

WestBow Press
A Division of Thomas Nelson & Zondervan
1663 Liberty Drive
Bloomington, IN 47403
www.westbowpress.com
1 (866) 928-1240

ISBN: 978-1-5127-2868-2 (sc)
ISBN: 978-1-5127-2869-9 (hc)
ISBN: 978-1-5127-2867-5 (e)

Library of Congress Control Number: 2016901447

Print information available on the last page.

WestBow Press rev. date: 02/23/2016

CONTENTS

ACKNOWLEDGMENTS

First, my lovely wife, who is a gift from God, deserves much more than a mere thanks. She has amazed me as she continues to turn the Word of God into flesh through her practice of walking in the footsteps of our Lord. To her, I owe much gratitude, because she has given me a deep thirst for the Living Water.

Also, my university mentor and friend, Dr. Steve Eckstein, gave me a desire for searching and researching the Word of God to know more and to be more like Jesus.

For the past half century, it has been my good fortune to dialogue with many outstanding scholars through their writings, which appear in the bibliography. They have led me into new corridors of thought and challenged me to rethink many concepts pertaining to the biblical message. Their writings pertinent to this monograph are listed in the bibliography.

PERSONAL BACKGROUND

My parents were believers in God and His Son, Jesus. That was the family culture in which I was raised. When I was thirteen, I was immersed in a horse tank with four feet of water to witness my belief in the death, burial, and resurrection of Jesus. There was not much understanding of the meaning of immersion; it was just the thing to do if you wanted to be saved.

When I was eighteen, I was medically discharged from the US Navy in March 1952. When I returned home, the semester at the university had already begun, so I had a few months until I could enroll in classes the next semester. This gave me the opportunity to immerse myself in a study of the gospels. My life would be forever transformed. Reading the Bible up to that point had been very casual, to say the least. Now, for the first time, when I read the gospel story, it was like a conversation with the author, God Himself. It quickly became apparent that what I was reading and discussing with God was very different from what I was hearing in sermons preached during Sunday worship. The substance or emphasis was not the same. What I was studying in the Gospels was about the Lord God, through His Son, bringing His kingdom to earth as it is in heaven. The promised new age had begun! And the amazing, almost unbelievable thing is that He wants me to be His partner. What I kept hearing from the pulpit was all about what I must do to be saved. The emphasis in the Bible is about what God is doing. The emphasis from the pulpit was what I should be doing—a narcissistic self-interest that is not the solution but the problem as stated in Genesis 3.[1] Seldom did I hear from the pulpit how I should be a partner with the Lord God to bring His kingdom to earth as it is in heaven.[2]

The next semester, I enrolled in several Bible courses and added a major in biblical studies to my business and economics major. One of the courses was Old Testament Survey taught by Dr. Steve Eckstein. What a revelation! I began to see that the sixty-six books of the Bible were not there to prove that my ideas were right but that they were a narrative revealing the world's most amazing story. I began to see that the story is about God's deep resolve to renew His beautiful creation to its

---

[1] After Eve's conversation with the serpent the conversation turned to self: I looked, I desired, and I ate.

[2] "your kingdom come, your will be done on earth as it is in heaven" (Matthew 6:10 NIV).

original grandeur after humanity was deceived by Satan and disobeyed God.

The first lesson I learned was to understand that not only is the Bible about history but also that it is written with other types of literary features, such as storylines, poetry, symbolism, and prophecy. For instance, the first eleven chapters, rather than giving historical particulars, develop a storyline or a plot that becomes more of God's problem in dealing with His rebellious creation.[3] The design is not to give insights into the geological structure of the earth nor a timeline about its age. Its design is to develop faith or trust in the Creator, a faith that presumes a merciful and gracious Lord God. Therefore, the first eleven chapters are not to be read historically, even though history is there, but

---

[3] See Bruggemann, *Genesis*.

they are to be read to say something about God and His vision.

The second lesson I learned was that the Bible was its best interpreter. This requires a belief that the words in the original manuscripts are "God-breathed" words. This doesn't mean that the words were dictated to the writer from God. Rather, it means that God saw someone who had the experiences, knowledge, and vocabulary who could write the story as God wanted. The Greek manuscripts use the word *theopneustos* to express this concept (2 Timothy 3:16). The correct translation of theopneustos is "God-breathed," the same idea used in Genesis 2:7 where God formed man from the dust of the earth and breathed into him the breath of life. We have become so used to the Latin Vulgate translation "inspired," which at best loses the influence of God. What if we used the same idea in Genesis 2:7?[4] Could we say that God inspired life in humanity, and they became alive? It simply is not the same as "God breathed" into his nostrils the breath of life. A football team can be inspired. Is this the same as if God breathed on the football team? No wonder the Word of God does not hold the absolute authority that it should. So since the Words of Life are "God-breathed," who can interpret those words better than the One who breathed them?

---

[4] "And the Lord God formed a man's body from the dust of the ground and breathed into it the breath of life" (NLT).

THE CREATION STORY

The creation story is introduced with a narrative about beginnings. Read Genesis 1 and 2 slowly and perceptively, as if the Lord God is talking to you. Notice the change in the order of "heaven and earth" in Genesis 1:1 and "earth and heaven" in Genesis 2:4. Why the change? It cannot be mere coincidence. The text in Genesis 1 is about God and creation. Notice that creation wasn't made as a carpenter makes a house. The created universe wasn't made but was spoken into existence. "Let there be light," He said. And He is still speaking to His creation. Communication with the Creator is part of the covenant He has made with His

1

creation. One way He does this is through His written Word. Another way is to observe those who turn His Word into flesh by walking according to His Word. Also, the creation was permitted to exist (Genesis 1:3, 6, 9, 11, 14, 15, 20, 24, 26). Genesis 2:4ff, the second creation story, is about earth and humankind. This explains something untold in Genesis 1. What is creation for? What is it about? What is it supposed to do for the reader? What is supposed to happen between the storyteller (God) and the reader (human)? Why did God push the waters back so dry land appeared? Is that significant for the plot of the biblical story? For instance, trace the land from Eden (Genesis 2) to Canaan (Genesis 12) to the world (Matthew 28) to "the sea is no more" (Revelation 21–22). Could that be a major theme of the biblical story? If it is, what does that change about our theology of going to heaven when we die? (By the way, going to heaven when we die is never mentioned in the biblical narrative.)[5]

Obviously God intended the dry land to be a place for God's flora and fauna and for His creatures, especially humans, to work the land.[6] It is a place where humankind can express the glory of God as the water covers the sea. The garden of Eden has been a source of misunderstanding for many Bible readers. We insist that Genesis 2:8 refers to a little spot in present-day Iraq, probably because of the mention of the Tigris and Euphrates Rivers. But read the text carefully. "And the Lord God planted a garden towards the east, in Eden." The question is east of what? The Bible is comprised of many different types of literature. It is not all literal history. There is history, but also poetry,

---

[5] See Wright's *Resurrection and the Son of God*, also *Surprised by Hope*.
[6] "The Lord God placed man in the Garden of Eden to tend and care for it" (NLT).

symbolism, and prophecy as well as story. You do not interpret history in the same way that you interpret poetry, prophecy, or symbolism.[7] If you took a picture of the garden, especially the two trees in the middle, what would appear on the negative? Obviously this is a storyline used to develop the plot of the biblical story. The emphasis is that the Lord God placed humans on the dry land He had created for humanity to live on. He had pronounced this land "good" or "beautiful," Eden, if you will. After all, *Eden* means "a place of delight." East doesn't always refer to direction only. Frequently it is east with rich symbolism meaning far more than direction only. This is the case here. East is also used to speak of the presence of God as in Ezekiel 43:2[8]; or righteousness as in Isaiah 41:2[9];

---

[7] See Davis and Hays, *The Art of Reading Scripture.*

[8] "Then the man brought me to the gate facing east, and I saw the glory of the God of Israel" (NIV).

[9] "Who has stirred up one from the east, calling him in righteousness to his service" (NIV).

or angels of God as in Revelation 7:27[10]. Similar ideas are included in the direction the Tabernacle and later the temple. They both faced toward the east. Why? Because that is toward the light of day. God is light (1 John 1:5).[11]

And what about the Tigris and Euphrates Rivers? Surely those who believe in the flood realize that rivers would change their course after such a deluge. After all, people in a new land often name things that were familiar in the old land. For instance, we have rivers in the United States with names from the old land that settlers were familiar with, such as the Thames in Connecticut, Severn in Maryland, and Trent in North Carolina. Additionally, note carefully the wording in chapter 2, verse 10. "Now a river went *out* of Eden to water the garden" (earth).

---

[10] "Then I saw another angel coming up from the east, having the seal of the living God" (NIV).

[11] "God is light and in Him there is no darkness at all" (NASV).

This was God's intent all along—for heaven (God's dimension) and earth (humanity's dimension) to work together. They are always created together, to be together, to work together.

Then there is the creation of humankind, which cries out for further study. Why create man and woman in God's likeness? First, as we shall see later, to take care of God's creation, that is to say, among other things, to be God's partner (servant) in caring for the garden (earth). What a glorious thought! What a privilege—being a servant to maintain God's handiwork! Second, humanity is to reflect the image of God. This seems to suggest fellowship, *koinonia*, a sharing of something similar, as well as being in covenant with God. Evidently, God intended a fourth member in what we usually think of as the Trinity. What does the "image" refer to and what does it mean? First, it has to do with character traits rather than function. As an example, God functions as the Father, He and He alone, not Jesus, not the Holy Spirit, and certainly not humanity. However, speaking of character, God is described as "kind." This also describes Jesus and the Holy Spirit, and it should describe humankind as they reflect the image of God. This seems to be what Paul had in mind in 2 Corinthians 3:18–19.[12] Certainly this was God's intent in Genesis 1:26, 27, 2:6, 7; that is, to have someone who shares the divine nature.[13] And humanity was created to do this as a servant or caretaker of God's creation (Genesis 2:5). This is the covenant between God

---

[12] "And all of us have had that veil removed so that we can be mirrors that brightly reflect the glory of the Lord. And as the Spirit of the Lord works in us, we become more and more like him and reflect his glory more and more"(NLT).

[13] "Through these he has given us his very great and precious promises, so that through them you may participate in the divine nature and escape the corruption in the world caused by evil desires"(2 Peter 1:4 NIV). One of the promises Peter is referring to in this statement must be the promised indwelling Holy Spirit who certainly was identical to God's nature.

and humankind—to share character traits, not function.

The covenant idea is so important that it required a second creation for humankind, that being a woman.[14] This special creation was to be a covenant between male and female, similar to the covenant between humanity and God. The woman was to be a partner to assist man, like the covenant between humankind and God, so that humanity could fully partner with God in presenting His image over all the earth. Notice the precise language in Genesis 1:27: "Male and female He created them." This is God's created order, and when humankind chooses to defy the divine order, they no longer reflect God's image but chooses to function in a way never intended by God.

---

[14] "Then the Lord God made a woman from the rib and brought her to Adam" (Genesis 2:22 NLT).

The consequence for that choice is death. God never created man to function as a woman, and He never created a woman to function as a man. Even the animal world understands the distinction. The consequences for that choice of men choosing to function as a woman or a woman choosing to function as a man is clearly revealed in Genesis 19:5–25:1. We have even coined a word for this outlandish choice (sodomy). The warning is even stronger against the choice of homosexuality in Romans 1:24–27.[15]

---

[15] "Therefore God gave them over in the sinful desires of their hearts to sexual impurity for the degrading of their bodies with one another. They exchanged the truth of God for a lie, and worshiped and served created things rather than the Creator—who is forever praised. Amen. Because of this God gave them over to shameful lusts. Even their women exchanged natural relation for unnatural ones. In the same way the men also abandoned natural relations with women and were inflamed with lust for one another. Men committed indecent acts with other men, and received in themselves the due penalty for their perversion" (NIV).

THE IMPORTANCE OF GENESIS 1-11

Why is this introductory interpretation important? First, it changes the emphasis from geological or temporal considerations to an emphasis on God and faith in Him. Second, it structures the storyline toward God's intent or vision and His deep resolve for His creation to be His glory and humanity's role to be His servant and thus share in His glory. Third, this view places heaven and earth, God and humanity, in concert rather than in conflict. Where there is conflict, it is not God's intent, and He is determined to resolve the tension. Yes, this is the focus of the biblical narrative from Genesis through Revelation. The focus of the biblical story is how

God intends to renew His good creation or the garden of Eden (earth) to its state before Genesis 3.

THE NARRATIVE BROADENS

The plot of the biblical story thickens into a melodrama in chapter 3 with the introduction of another character, namely the deceiver. How will humanity, created in God's image, manage the choice between being a servant and a desire for something else (being like God)? Yet, there is a more profound question for the biblical story, that being how will God deal with the deceiver?[16] The dramatic conversation between the serpent and Eve, with its aftermath, is one of many biblical scenes misunderstood and thus misinterpreted by a great number of Bible readers. To think of it as "the fall of humankind," as it is frequently interpreted,

---

[16] See Brueggemann's *Genesis.*

gets us on the wrong track of the main theme of the biblical story. The emphasis in the story is not "the fall of humankind" but the grace and mercy of God. How does God handle the insubordination of His creation? That is the question the biblical story addresses.

So what has happened to the covenant between God and His creation? How is it possible that humanity created in God's image could defy partnership with God? Look at the text carefully. Up to this point, the words used to reference God are YHWH Elohim (Genesis 2:4, 5, 7, 8, 9, 15, 16, 18, 19, 21, 22, 3:1). The deceiver changes that to Elohim only in chapter 3:2. God is no longer Almighty God, but to him, just one god among many, and a selfish one at that (Genesis 3:4, 5). This gets us to the heart of the problem. Humanity in the image of God is free to choose. We can follow whomever we please—God or the deceiver. The storyline is cast. Notice what happens when Eve chooses to follow the deceiver. Eve saw that the tree was good for food and delightful to look at and something to make one wise (Genesis 3:6). Notice the thinking. It is about self, not God. When we stop talking to God and begin talking about Him concerns about our self soon begin to dominate our thoughts. So she consumed and broke partnership with God and partnered with the deceiver. The problem fleshed out has become a desire to be like God— not only in character but also in function. In doing so, ironically, humanity abrogated His authority over all creation (Genesis 3:6). The text clearly states the consequences of this foolish choice. God's creatures no longer have an interest in the garden. Now it is only about them. "I saw. I desired. I ate. I was naked. I was afraid" (Genesis 3:10). The garden is ignored. The covenant between God and humankind is broken. The pain in God's heart is so deep that words cannot describe.

What is God to do? How will His wonderful vision of creation come to fruition? The die is cast for the rest of the biblical story. First, the magnificent grace of God becomes even more evident. It is revealed in Genesis 3:15 but now is emphasized again by removing humanity from the garden, that is to say, from the presence and glory of God (Ichabod as in 1 Samuel 4:21–22).[17] This is a gracious act of God because it keeps them from living a life separated from God forever. The wording is telling in 3:24: "So God drove out the man; and He placed at the east of the garden of Eden the cherubim and a flaming sword which turned every way to keep and guard the way to the tree of life." The sentence is severe

---

[17] "And she named the child Ichabod, saying, The glory is departed from Israel; because the ark of God was taken" (KJV).

but not as severe as promised. But it does reveal a true definition of death, that being separation from God. Notice the wording in Genesis 3:24. Why place the cherubim and flaming sword at the east if not to suggest a separation from God? Isaiah explained the reason for the separation in chapter 59 verse 2, "Your disobedience has separated you from your God."[18] God promised death yet they did not die a physical death. However, they were separated from the source of life which the casting out symbolized. The cherubim and flaming sword are elegant symbols testifying to the severity of disobedience. Perhaps this is a revelation of God's grace. He doesn't wish anyone to partake of the tree of life and live forever separated from His love.

The question is, "Why can't humankind be content with reflecting God's image without desiring to

---

[18] The author's rendition of the text.

function like God?" The desire to function like God becomes the essence of sin, and God is determined to remedy this problem. It will take a long, long time, but God's resolve and love are deep. But we must go deeper than the standard view of merely erasing "sin" from the ledger or simply viewing baptism (immersion) as "washing away my sins" as true as that concept is. This view does not get to the heart of the problem, that being a change in heart or a new heart and also an indwelling new spirit.[19] Nor does it remove the reason for estrangement from God. The nucleus of the problem is a desire to be like God. Until that desire is removed, sin still lies at the door. Maybe this explains why there are so many stillborn births at baptism. Sins are washed away, but we still see sin as something to be desired or "good, delightful to look at, and desired

---

[19] Peter replied, "Repent and be baptized, every one of you, in the name of Jesus Christ for the forgiveness of your sins. And you will receive the gift of the Holy Spirit" (Acts 2:38 NIV).

to make one wise." So, like Eve, we take and eat. It also means that we have not received the Holy Spirit, the breath of God that gives new life which is essential to life for the newborn. Without the reception of the Holy Spirit, we are stillborn.

David understood the principle long ago when he prayed, "Create in me a clean heart and place a renewed spirit within me" (Psalm 51:10). Notice, he is praying for a new creation with a new spirit. That is the essence of what Jesus came to do. Later Paul suggested a similar view when he wrote, "Therefore if any anyone is in Christ (king), he is a new creation, the old is gone, the new has come."[20] Jesus remarked, "Whatever comes out of the mouth comes from the heart, and this is what makes man unclean" (Matthew 15:18ff). The principle is rooted deep in the Old Testament in the

---

[20] 2 Corinthians 5:17 (NIV).

Shema (Deuteronomy 6:5). The law, the principal of which is still in effect, states, "You must love the Lord your God with all your heart, with all your soul, with all your strength and mind" (Mark 12:30). Again, unless this new heart is created by being born anew,[21] and the Holy Spirit is given at the new birth,[22] the immersed one is stillborn and continues to be separated from God. Just as the natural human needs spirit for life, so the new born-again human needs the Holy Spirit to be a living person in the kingdom of God. If not, the old desire to be like God is still there. If a human is resurrected with a new heart, the desire to function like God is gone, and a satisfaction in reflecting God's image becomes his or her goal. The person then understands his or her function of being a partner,

---

[21] "Jesus answered and said to him, "Truly, truly, I say to you, unless one is born again he cannot see the kingdom of God" (John 3:3 NAS).

[22] "Peter replied, "Each of you must turn from your sins and turn to God, and be baptized in the name of Jesus Christ for the forgiveness of your sins. Then you will receive the gift of the Holy Spirit"(Acts 2:38 NLT).

caretaker, and servant, and the newborn human delights in that function. The image of God is then reflected more accurately.[23] We seem to never get the point that is illustrated time and again in the biblical story. Being first makes us last, and being a servant makes us first (Cain/Abel; Esau/Jacob; and Ishmael/Isaac).

The proper function of God's created ones is clearly stated in Matthew 20:26, "Whoever wishes to be great must be a servant." The example is beautifully stated in Philippians 2:6: "Although being one with God He did not think equality with God was a thing to be grasped, but He assumed the guise of a servant."[24] When God created humanity in His image, He was referring only to characteristics, not function.

---

[23] "And we all, with unveiled face, beholding the glory of the Lord are being transformed into the same image from one degree of glory to another"(2 Corinthians 3:18 ESV).

[24] (AB).

When God created humankind in His image, one trait given to humanity was freedom to choose. God did not make a robot. He created humankind in His image. In the garden of Eden, God gave humanity a choice with a prohibition. You may not eat of the tree of knowledge of good and evil (Genesis 2:7). It is interesting that there was no prohibition pertaining to the tree of life. The intriguing question is, "Why did Adam and Eve choose death when they could have choosen life?" This choice is the center of the entire biblical story—life or death. That was the deception of the serpent (Satan). He insisted that knowledge of good and evil was not death but life. You'll be like God. Gods don't die; they live.

The tree of knowledge of good and evil is never referred to again in the biblical story with actual words, but the principle is always there. So is the choice! Try to function as God, and death awaits. Ask Abraham (Genesis 12:17–20). Ask Isaac (Genesis 26:9). Ask Jacob (Genesis 27:41). Ask Moses (Exodus 2:14). Ask Israel when they were in exile. It remained a choice when Israel settled in Canaan (Deuteronomy 11:26–29). The prophets knew the consequences of choosing for self rather than God (Isaiah 7:16; Jeremiah 8:3). But in spite of humankind's erroneous choice, God's relentless resolve to recreate His lovely creation remained steadfast. His grace never ceases nor does His enduring love for His creation.

The desire to renew His creation must have been heart wrenching for God. Never overlook the effect that humankind's disobedience had on a gracious Father. "Now the Lord observed the extent of the people's wickedness, and He saw that all their thoughts were consistently and totally evil. So the

Lord was sorry He had ever made them. It broke His heart. And the Lord said, 'I will destroy all the animals and birds, too. I am sorry I ever made them.'" [25]

---

[25] Genesis 6:5–7 (NLT).

THE FLOOD NARRATIVE

"And God said to Noah, I intend to destroy all flesh and the land."[26] A flood came, and water covered the earth. Everyone on the earth perished. But please note: the earth remained. Cleansed, renewed, for sure, but God's created earth remained. Genesis 6–9 is a foretaste of another renewal mentioned in 2 Peter 3:5–13. Peter even compares this renewal to the Genesis flood in verses 6–7.[27] Similar to the cleansing with water but different since this

---

[26] "And God said to Noah, 'I have determined to make an end of all flesh, for the earth is filled with violence. Behold, I will destroy them with the earth'" (Genesis 6:13 ESV; see also AB).

[27] "Through which the world that then existed was deluged with water and perished. But by the same word the present heavens and earth have been stored up for fire, being kept until the Day of Judgment and destruction of the ungodly people."

cleansing is with fire. Fire is another cleansing agent (Malachi 3:2; Matthew 3:10–12; 1 Corinthians 3:13). However, this time there will be new heavens and a new earth in which humanity's desire to be like God is forever changed (2 Peter 3:13). Contrary to the popular interpretation of 2 Peter 3, the earth remains after this purging, just as it remained after the purging in Genesis 6. Changed, renewed, recreated, a very definite yes; but not annihilated, gone forever as the Greek philosophers believed. Interpreting 2 Peter 3 with the beautiful earth, the garden of God's delight, destroyed leads to a Platonic view of life after the resurrection.[28] This is a belief of disembodied spirits dwelling in a false view of heaven. This belief hardly embraces a created, bodily human reflecting God's image. Also, it is a denial of a bodily resurrection clearly

---

[28] See Wright, *The Resurrection of the Son of God.*

taught throughout the Bible and exemplified by the resurrection of Christ.

The flood narrative presents another portrait of God's struggle in responding to the calloused hearts of humankind. Through Noah, God will avert the sorry state of human alienation. The narrative suggests again the interaction between heaven and earth (Genesis 6:1–4). But the interaction isn't as it should be. Notice the language. The image of God is exchanged for lust. Even though this is in a different arena of human existence, that being sex, it is very much the same as Eve's lust or desire to please self. It's all about what I want, not what God wants. "The sons of God saw that the daughters of man were fair. They then took what they desired." This is the same language used by Eve in Genesis 3:6. The consequences of this self- centered action was a shortening of life, yet with grace. However, the focus of the flood narrative is not about the flood. It is about the change in God in His dealing with the desire in humanity's hearts that leads to alienation from God. To say it another way, the story is not concerned with historical data, even though it is there, but with the strange things that happen in God's heart that affect His creation. The narrative is about God and His peculiar way of transforming or renewing His creation.

God will not abandon His vision for His magnificent creation. The narrative doesn't present Him as the angered Creator but more as a disappointed, hurt parent. Think of Jesus as He approached Jerusalem for the last time (Matthew 23; Luke 13). He sobbed because people were rejecting Him as God's long promised King of His Kingdom. What God saw in the hearts of humanity also hurt His great heart. This is also a heart-to-heart occasion.

"It grieved God that He had made man." There is no grief compared to that. The evil heart of humankind troubles the compassionate heart of a Father.

What is He to do? There is something deeply wrong with humankind. God's vision, His dream for His creation, has no prospect of fulfillment. Again, the emphasis in the flood text is not so much about the terrible consequences of the flood as it is about the painful crisis in how God will deal with His wayward creation. He is decisively impacted by the suffering and hurt of His creation. And He enters into the world's hurt and heals it, renews it through suffering. This is also a prelude to how His Son enters into the world's hurt bringing healing and renewal through His suffering on Golgotha that also inaugurated a new world. In this dismal story of pain and suffering, there is one who embodies a new possibility. Something new is at work in the suffering of God.

The newness is explained without fanfare in Genesis 8:20. "And Noah built an altar to the Lord and took of every clean animal and of every clean bird and offered burnt offerings on the altar." What kind of offering was this? It was a burnt offering. The main aspect of the burnt offering is that the entire animal was offered on the altar, suggesting a total commitment of the person offering the sacrifice.[29] Nothing like it has been mentioned in the text before. What does it say about Noah? Is this the man as God created him to be? Well, yes. Has God's suffering worked a miracle in the heart of man? Again, yes.

---

[29] "And the priest shall burn all of it on the altar, as a burnt offering, a food offering with a pleasing aroma to the Lord" (Leviticus 1:9 ESV). Also see Exodus 29:18.

An offering or sacrifice says something about the one who offers the sacrifice. In this case, since the entire offering was burned (Genesis 29:18 uses the same language in its effect on God; that is, sweet fragrance), the suggestion is that everything I am or have I give to you, my Almighty God. That is total commitment. That is humanity functioning as God created them to function. It is humanity reflecting the image of God in thanksgiving. This is the renewed world as God intended.

So what does the flood narrative teach? What is the inherent principle? God resolves that He will stay with His creation notwithstanding their wayward hearts. He will not allow their rebellion to sway Him from His grand dream. He will create new heavens and a new earth! The flood has affected no change in human hearts, as we will soon see, but it has affected an irreversible change in God.

God will deal firmly and justly with His creation, but with patience. It is now clear. That path will be a pathway of untold suffering and cost to God. He has made a decision. His creation will become as He wished through His own grief and suffering or, if you will, through His own burnt offering. But humankind's calloused hearts do not have the last word. God still presides over His creation. "I will remember my covenant promise" (Genesis 9:15). The sign of the covenant between God and the earth was the rainbow (Genesis 9:17). It remains to this day.

Now you would think that this would convince humanity to be the kind of people God created them to be. But you would be wrong. Their hearts, their desires for self, haven't changed. Soon after the flood, the selfish desire in humankind's hearts surfaced again. "They spoke the same language and began to talk about a construction project. Wasn't God's construction good enough? They said let's build a great tower, a great monument to ourselves. This will keep us together."[30] What? A tower to keep us together. What about allegiance to God keeping humankind together? Sounds very modern to me as we promote program after program for ourselves but push God further and further out of our lives. So God gave them different languages, and they were scattered over the earth. The irony of this is that, in the beginning, God wanted humankind to multiply and fill the earth. God's purpose will be done in spite of humanity's folly! It wasn't until the day of Pentecost in Acts 2 that they began to understand each other again.

---

[30] "Now the whole earth used the same language and the same words. It came about as they traveled east, that they found a plain in the land of Shinar and settled there. They said to one another, 'Come, let us make bricks and burn them thoroughly.' And they used brick for stone, and they used tar for mortar. They said, 'Come, let us build for ourselves a city, and a tower whose top will reach into heaven, and let us make a name for ourselves, otherwise we will be scattered abroad over the face of the whole earth'" (Genesis 11:1–4 NASB).

But that is in the new world and for another time. However, God's response was to take a completely new tactic to change the calloused hearts of humanity.

THE ABRAHAM NARRATIVE

(Genesis 11:27–25:18)

Two questions appear in this narrative for investigation. How does this narrative move the story of God's deep resolve to restore His beautiful creation forward? How does it relate to the first eleven chapters of Genesis? This narrative is where the biblical story begins with specific details about humankind's response to the grace of God. It follows the introduction, which establishes the plot of the story in Genesis 1–11. The text is pivotal and is frequently referred to as the story unfolds. It is a link between the providential care of God reflected in the call of Abram to a second call, the call of Israel, and finally a third call of disciples to follow Jesus that appears in the gospels. This is finally followed by a larger call for all followers of Jesus, His disciples (*ekklesia*), or those called out. The call always asks those who are called to be blessings to others. Through Abraham's call His seed would bless all people. Through the call of Israel God would become known throughout the world. The disciples call would make them fishers of men. The call is about caring for God's creation; that is, telling the marvelous story of what God has done through His Son (created believers anew) so that His image might be reflected over the entire earth. The call of God is similar to the speech God used to "create" the heavens and earth. The point is that God is always engaged in and with His creation.

Significantly, the call of Abram in Genesis 12 has striking similarities to the call of Adam and Eve in chapters 2–3. God is leading His family to a land later described as "a land flowing with milk and honey" (Exodus 3:8; Deuteronomy 6:3), or another delightful land, a garden of Eden. In fact, in Genesis 13:10, Canaan is described as being like the "garden of the Lord." Abram's mission is also very similar to Adam's and Eve's; that is, to care for God's creation, more specifically to be a blessing to all families of the earth. There are also blessings or curses depending on the choices made. Actually this is very similar to the two trees portrayed in the garden of Eden—death or curses if the image of God is not reflected (Genesis 12:3); blessings whenever or wherever God's image is reflected. To emphasize again, the call was not only for Abram. It was a call to be a reflection of God's image so that the entire earth would be blessed.

Additionally, very similar to Genesis 3 where God walked in the garden, God appeared to Abram in this garden (Canaan) also. The point being that heaven (God) and earth (humanity) are always together. God didn't create the heavens and earth and then leave them to go on their own way. Heaven and earth belong together. God's sphere (heaven) and humanity's sphere (earth) are created to be one.[31] That is God's vision, and He is determined that one day heaven and earth will be merged together forever. What a moment that will be!

But the question remains. Why Canaan? If you observed a map of that time and located Canaan in relation to other countries, what would you see? Canaan would be at the center of human travel routes for that part of the world at that time. It

---

[31] "Thus says the Lord; 'Heaven is my throne, and earth is my footstool'" (Isaiah 66:1 ESV). See also Ps 89, 115, 119.

would be the ideal place for those carrying the image of God to influence others. For instance, if you wished to travel from Haran to Egypt, the obvious route to take would be through Canaan. What an ideal place to reflect God's image and be a blessing to all nations! The intervention of God's providence in human affairs cannot be overlooked.

The Abraham narrative with its covenant blessings introduces a movement in the biblical story the importance of which can hardly be overstated. From father Abraham to son Isaac to grandson Jacob to great grandson Joseph, the constant watch of God over His creation and the wise choices of creation as well as foolish, selfish choices all with corresponding consequences are clearly stated in the narrative from Genesis 12 to Genesis 50. Even though this time period that we frequently refer to as the patriarchal period is comparatively short—about six hundred years covering four generations—there are a number of salient points to consider that are frequently referred to in the biblical story.

Of paramount importance is the constant presence of God communicating with and directing the affairs of His creation. When Abram was ninety-nine years old, the Almighty God appeared and said (notice the similarity to Genesis 1), "Walk habitually before me and I will make a covenant with you."

The covenant, which was amazingly not between equals, was a conditional vow or promise. Proper choices were of the essence. God's promise in the covenant was similar to Genesis 1:28, that being, "I will provide." Humankind's part of the covenant was to reflect God's image through service. This was to be a habitual covenant (Genesis 28:13–15; Exodus 24:7; Isaiah 55:3–5).

IMPLICATIONS OF THE COVENANT

The text detailing the four generations from Abram to Joseph exposes the danger and struggle of faith. However, God is always present and directing the affairs of His creation. Two questions of faith arise. Will God keep His outlandish promises? And will God's creatures trust Him? Will Abraham and Sarai trust the promise, or will they take the promise and, unwilling to wait on God, do their own thing? Will Jacob trust in God's promises, or will he continue to connive according to his own will? Trusting in God is never without doubts or other difficulties. For instance, for Abraham, the Promised Land is famine land and requires contact with other nations. In Jacob's case, he has to deal with the trickery of a prospective father-in-law. When they act faithlessly, curses are released in the land. The question is always there. Can Abram be trusted with the covenant? Can God be trusted?

The sign of the covenant was circumcision. With this sign, Abram's name was changed to Abraham, meaning "father of a multitude." Circumcision identified someone who believed (trusted) God and reflected His image by his lifestyle. However, the sign soon became a problem, rather than a symbol of a covenant blessing. Rather than circumcision being a sign of a cut or broken heart as well as a sign of submission, it became an item within itself. Circumcision took on a life within itself. Having the symbol became of first importance. What it signified, submission to God, became secondary. Humankind was back where they started, wanting to be like God, wanting to function like God rather than reflecting His character. Circumcision was to be a fleshly symbol of a circumcised heart. A circumcised heart is the true essence of humankind's part of the covenant.

GOD'S PROVIDENCE THROUGH FOUR GENERATIONS

The promise of land and the promise of a son becomes a key to God's provision during the six hundred years between God's call to Abram and the move to Egypt because of a great famine. This is the second move of God's chosen ones from Canaan to Egypt. Obviously, this is God's doing. Abraham's greatness becomes apparent because of his trust in the promise when there is no apparent evidence to support the promise. In fact, the evidence of old age and famine in the chosen land are both against trust or belief in the promise. Yet Abraham believed, and it was counted as righteousness (Romans 4).

It is interesting that the birth of the son, Isaac, has similarities to the birth of another Son, Jesus. Both are the result of God's intervention into human affairs. God's resolve to bring His creation back on course to the fulfillment of His vision in Genesis 1–2 is everywhere evident. Humanly speaking, to go to a land where God leads and find a famine or to hear a promise of a son when you are in your nineties and to continue to trust are marvels in themselves. But this is characteristic of the four generations we call patriarchs. In spite of their humanness, they are sterling examples of reflecting God's image. There is no indication they tried to convert their neighbors. Yet, by the way they lived, their neighbors knew and feared YHWH (Genesis 26:28; 28:15; 39:2–6).

A very important principle guiding these four generations was their cognizance of the constant presence of God and His intervention in their lives. For example, in Genesis 18 before God destroyed Sodom and Gomorrah, Abraham had lived so close to God that God felt it was important to share His plan to destroy the cities. Thus, Psalm 37:5 epitomizes Abraham's life: "Commit your way to the Lord; trust in Him and He will act."

Isaac sought a wife under the provision of God (Genesis 24). Her name was to be Rebekah. And when Isaac prayed to God on her behalf for children, God not only answered his prayer but also continued the promise of land. Again, as with Abraham, there was a son and a land of promise. Whenever Rebekah intervened to get the second-born son blessed instead of the firstborn, Esau, the mysterious intervention of God became powerfully evident. Obviously God saw something in them even before they were born. Like Jeremiah in Jeremiah 1, God knew them even before they were born. The covenant continues even in spite of human weakness. God will not be dissuaded of His vision for His creation. Humans cannot function like gods. Their role is always to reflect God's image.

It is interesting that whenever Jacob faced difficulty, usually of his own making, God interceded. Heaven and earth merged together to advance God's purpose for His creation. In Genesis 28, God came to Jacob in a dream when he was seeking a wife. God renewed the promise of land that had been given to his grandfather Abraham and his father, Isaac. Here again, heaven and earth partner together.

When Jacob was to meet his brother, Esau, to reconcile years of bitterness and hatred, heaven and earth converged again. A tremendous wrestling between God and Jacob ensued (Genesis 32).

This striving with God resulted in a significant name change that God had been working to accomplish for many years. Jacob means "to supplant." Israel means "one who strives with God." The name, Israel, also suggests in Hebrew, one over whom God has mastery. Hebrew words with the initials EL refers to Elohim, one of the names for God. It is another way of saying, "My people are those who reflect my image." The biography of Jacob, now Israel, changes from this event onward. Whenever Israel was true to its name, it was blessed exceedingly. When it was untrue to the name, curses ensued.

The constant presence of God and His intervention in human affairs are evident in the Joseph narrative

(Genesis 37–50). This narrative continues a principle well known to the biblical reader by now. That principle is "the last shall be first." Jacob, being the last born himself, had lived this principle and experienced the results through heartaches, as he learned to be a servant of God. He also experienced blessings as well, blessings beyond measure, after his wrestling with God. The question then becomes, what is the purpose of "the last shall be first"? Is it not to emphasize that this is why God created humankind—to be a servant—and when humanity serves, humanity is reflecting the image of God? The only begotten Son of God, Himself who served, is the epitome of the principle (Philippians 2). In one sense, He was the second man as well as the last Adam (1 Corinthians 15:45–49). Follow Him (Matthew 16:24; John 10:4)! Through His service, He became first and amazingly made us first, when we become servants as He was.

Also, the Joseph narrative continues the speaking of God to His chosen ones. There, of course, was no God-breathed written word, but God still speaks to His creation. Again, the speech comes through dreams. Jacob heard the voice through dreams. Now God speaks to Joseph. He always has spoken to His chosen, and He always will. But His chosen must listen carefully and decipher. Why don't we expect the One Who spoke the heavens and earth into existence to continue to speak to His chosen? More important still, why don't we listen?

The dream episode exposes a principle that rings true today. Those who don't dream regard dreams as absurd. Just as those who don't study God's speech today think the words of God are absurd. As in Genesis 11, "They do not listen." But this doesn't deter God from His passion of renewing His creation as He envisioned in Genesis 1 and 2.

Joseph's brothers, who became jealous of a colored coat, now allow jealousy to turn into hatred because of a dream. They vented their wrath against Joseph by selling him to distant relatives, the Ishmaelites, remember Ishmael and Isaac, who in turn sold him to the Egyptians. But notice the providence of God at work. A famine in Canaan caused Joseph's family to move to Egypt where there was abundance due to God's chosen servant, Joseph, taking care of His garden. Who could have imagined that Egypt would turn into Eden, a land of delight? Where God is present, the impossible becomes possible. Only Joseph knew the truth by saying to his brothers, "You meant it for evil, but God meant it for good." Here we are confronted with the core of biblical truth. God works newness in spite of human folly.

In Genesis 45, Joseph perceives God's hand in the unfolding events. Three times he says, "God sent me." In verse 5, he said, "God sent me to preserve life." This has always been God's intent for His chosen ones. He calls and is present, not only for the sake of those called but also so that through them others might be blessed. In verse 7 Joseph says, "God sent me before you to preserve for you a remnant." He emphasizes God's hand in these events by saying, "It was not you who sent me but God; and He has made me father, lord, and ruler" (verse 8).

Even as the Genesis record comes to a conclusion in the Joseph narrative, it is not the end but merely the beginning of the greatest story ever told as the name Genesis suggests. The events surrounding the exodus speak eloquently of God's resolve to reclaim His creation for His original purpose, that being to reflect His image.

THE EXODUS NARRATIVE

First, it is important to remember that at this time, Egypt was the most powerful nation on earth. In many respects, this makes the exodus event a marvel. It reaffirms that God truly is engaged in the affairs of His chosen people. As Paul averred in Romans 8:28,[32] God is working to accomplish His purpose for His creation whether His intervention is obvious or not. This is the first face-to-face contest between the kingdom of this world and the kingdom of God. It will not be the last.

---

[32] "And we know that God causes all things to work together for good to those who love God, to those who are called according to his purpose" (NASB).

The seminal events of the exodus, which means "the way out," includes but is not limited to Moses and his call; the contest between Moses and pharaoh's priests; the plagues; Passover and firstborn; Red Sea, sometimes referred to as Reed Sea; Sinai and promise of land; establishment of covenant; and the tent or meeting place. These events were to form Israel into a people who reflected God's image in their lives. All of them were to open a way to God's heart and develop trust in Him as Israel's king. God's leadership provided a true model for all of Israel's kings and gave a foretaste of the coming Lord of Lords and King of Kings (Isaiah 40; Psalm 23; Psalm 93).

Episodes in the life of Moses indicate the providential intervention of God as He continued His resolve to have His creation as He envisioned in Genesis 1 and 2. Evidently God saw in Moses qualities that could move this climatic chapter in humanity forward. However, just as with all of us, training, discipline, and actual experiences with God were necessary before Moses was prepared to serve God in this extraordinary manner. These events were recorded in Exodus 1–20. Of course, the training continued all of Moses' life, encompassing 120 years from his unusual birth to his death as disclosed in Deuteronomy 34. Deuteronomy 33 expresses, in a phenomenal manner, the result of 120 years walking and talking with God. What a view of a true spokesman of God!

Notice the statement given to Moses by God as he stood before Pharaoh. "Israel is my firstborn son. Let my son go that he may worship me."[33] This is the first biblical statement referring to humans as God's children. This no doubt sets the stage for a

---

[33] Exodus 4:22–23.

true Son as in Matthew 2:15, "out of Egypt I called my Son," or in Matthew 3:17, "This is my Son in whom I am well pleased." In short, Jesus was the Son that God wanted Israel to be. The purpose was, going back to Abraham, to be a blessing to all. In essence, this is the true purpose of the exodus—the way out of bondage to freedom in the Promised Land. Significantly, this is what Moses and Elijah were discussing in Luke 9:30–31.[34] The Greek word they used translates "departure" as in "exodus." In other words, Jesus leads humanity in a true exodus. This time not out of Egypt but what Egypt symbolized out of a deeper slavery, that being sin or anything that separates us from God.[35]

---

[34] "Two men, Moses and Elijah, appeared in glorious splendor, talking with Jesus. They spoke about his departure, which he was about to bring to fulfillment at Jerusalem."

[35] "Behold, the Lord's hand is not shortened, that it cannot save, or his ear dull, that it cannot hear; but your iniquities have made a separation between you and your God, and your sins have hidden his face from you so that he does not hear"(Isaiah 59:1–2 ESV).

The astonishing change in the relationship between God and Israel, especially Israel's representative, Jesus, is almost indescribable. Before, to see God meant death (Exodus 19:21). Now it is, "Those who have seen me have seen the Father" (John 14:9) and "the Father and I are one" (John 10:30). It used to be, "Don't touch or you will die" (Exodus 19:12). Now it is, "Don't you realize that you are God's temple?" (1 Corinthians 6:19). And above all, Jesus taught us to pray to God as "Father" (Matthew 6:9). It is interesting that the word Jesus used, usually translated "heaven" is plural (*heavens*) as it is in Genesis 1:1 and 2:4. This helps to understand the difficult passage in 2 Corinthians 12:2 about the third heaven (singular).[36] This was a Jewish way of speaking about the presence of God. However, the word translated "heaven" in Matthew 6:10 (*ourano*)

---

[36] "I know a man in Christ who fourteen years ago was caught up to the third heaven" (NIV).

is singular, suggesting a merging of heaven and earth where God and His image (man) are one. The plural used in Matthew 6:9 (*ouranois*)[37] emphasizes the presence of God everywhere (heavens) whereas the singular used in Matthew 6:10 focuses His presence on earth, the domain of humankind.

The intimacy between God and His creation is so loving, so beautiful. This is what God envisioned in Genesis 1 and 2 when He said, "Let us make a man in our image, like us." Exodus is the initial God-driven act that would see its fulfillment in His renewed earth.[38]

---

[37] Barbara and Timothy Friberg, eds., *Analytical Greek New Testament* (Grand Rapids: Baker Book House, 1981), 16–17.

[38] "For behold, I create new heavens and a new earth, and the former things shall not be remembered or come to mind." 2 Peter 3:13 "But according to His promise we are waiting for new heavens and a new earth in which righteousness dwells" (Isaiah 65:17 ESV).

The exodus event also discloses the conflict between the kingdom of God and the kingdoms of the world (Psalm 10:10). The victory of God over the kingdoms of the world is repeated so often in the biblical narrative that our faith should be unshakable. Think of the victories not just over Egypt but also the victories in Palestine over other kingdoms as told in the narratives of Joshua and Judges, not to mention the victories mentioned in Kings and Chronicles, and last but not least, the victory over the Babylonians and, finally, over Rome itself.

And the most marvelous victory of all was the victory over death itself! The verdict is in, especially in Jesus' conversation with Pilate: "You have no power except what is given you by my Father." Finally, look at Luke's grand disclosure at the end of Acts where God's messenger Paul is at the heart of the Roman Empire, preaching the victory of the true King, Christ. Luke's statement of God to Paul in Acts 27:24, "You must stand before Caesar," is almost identical to a parallel declaration to Moses in Exodus 3:10, "I will send you to Egypt." Luke is saying as well as words can that God's kingdom is now on earth just as it was when He called Israel out of Egypt! Both men were sent to be God's representative to empires which were opposed to the Kingdom of God. In fact, Egypt became a synonym for evil. Rome became a synonym for Babylon, a place of captivity for God's people. Both Moses and Paul were messengers of God to proclaim the Kingdom of God to empires which did not accept His authority.

Let's look at the initial act of God in leading His people out of slavery to freedom in the Promised Land as told in Exodus 7–12 commonly called the ten plagues. The plagues described as the "powerful and outstretched arm of the Lord" put the world on notice for all time that YHWH is not only Creator but also that He is Lord of His creation. It is worth noting that the first three plagues affected the Israelites as well as the Egyptians. During plagues four through nine only the Egyptians were affected. What would Israel think?

What would the Egyptians think when they saw the plagues affecting them and not touching the Israelites? Surely the question on all lips would be, "Why?" Obviously they were to increase Israel's faith or trust in God. The verification of their effect is disclosed in the tenth plague. "The blood will be a sign for you on the houses where you are; and when I see the blood, I will pass over you" (Exodus 12:13 NIV). The pertinent question is, what did God see in the blood? Another related question must also be asked. What was the Israelite thinking when he killed the lamb and put the blood on the door posts? No one had ever been asked to do such a thing before. These questions are not trivial or meaningless. They are the same scenario we face in God's presence every day of our life. Remember: Israel had just experienced nine plagues over a short time. The plagues resulted in growing faith and knowledge of YHWH as the true God. Would you obey God under these circumstances? I suggest what God saw was not only the blood (life) of an innocent animal but also the growing faith in the heart of the Israelite. This also has significance when we gather around the communion table and partake of the symbolic blood of our Passover Lamb.

Did the Israelite have any feelings for the lamb whose blood became the source of redemption for him or her and the Israelite's household? Would the thought that the lamb died instead of the Israelite cross his or her mind? Though any answer to these questions cannot be proven beyond doubt, I suggest that a rational answer would be a resounding yes they would have feelings of remorse. Remorse because a pure, spotless lamb was dying on their behalf. These, and more, are issues Paul addresses in 1 Corinthians 5:7 when he said, "Christ (the King), our Passover Lamb, has been sacrificed." Remember: God is preparing His people for citizenship in the Promised Land. Obedience, humility, and sorrow are necessary traits for dwelling in the Promised Land. In Matthew 5:7, Christ said, "Blessed are those who mourn because they will be comforted." He said this to stipulate one of the necessary characteristics of God's people living in the new age. This, of course, follows the blessedness of "being poor in spirit."

Paul's version in 2 Corinthians 7:10 reiterates the same message, "Godly sorrow leads to repentance."

These characteristics, expressed by both Christ (the King) and Paul, are therefore essential qualities of membership in the kingdom of God, suggested by the deliverance of Israel from Egypt and fully realized by the resurrection of Jesus that was the victory over the last enemy, death itself. With His resurrection, the new creation had begun, in this case, a new age with a new world and a new humanity that will be fully consummated when He returns. This, and more, was foreshadowed in the exodus event. It speaks eloquently of the enduring love of God and should develop faith in His created ones. If not, why not? All other alternatives are dead ends.

As God's now chosen firstborn son, Israel, departs from the land of slavery to the land of freedom, it soon discovers that to be chosen by God involved a transformation of character. That transformation is encompassed in what we call "law." But the law was always to teach who God was and how to live as His people and reflect His image to the world. The law was a pathway to freedom and the heart of God. It is important that the law was written on two tablets. Why? Because this is a covenant between two parties. The symbolism is that each party receives a copy of the law. This is similar to our duplicate copies today. To obey the law always led to blessings. To disobey always led to disaster, which, in essence, was a violation and affront to the Lawgiver Himself.

Interesting that the law always pointed to the Lawgiver. To make the point of who Israel was representing, the Lawgiver lived in their midst. God dwelt in their midst. By the way, this is the same word used by John when he said in his gospel that the Word became flesh and dwelt among us full of grace and truth. The law, when obeyed, in reality, developed Israel into a nation with God as its king. The implication of a new king, a new creation, and a new nation is evident in Exodus 24:15–17.[39] This is very suggestive of the creation story in Genesis 1–2. But this would be a nation with a difference, different because their king was, in fact, the Creator of the cosmos, and not only Creator but also Lord as evidenced in Egypt, and He will continue to be Lord as Israel occupies the Promised Land. In other words, YHWH was not to be viewed as one god among many. He was the One and only God. Additionally, He was a king

---

[39] "When Moses went up on the mountain, the cloud covered it, and the glory of the Lord settled on Mount Sinai. For six days the cloud covered the mountain, and on the seventh day the Lord called to Moses from within the cloud. To the Israelites the glory of the Lord looked like a consuming fire."

who could be loved as a father just as the Shema[40] taught and as Jesus made clear when He came (Matthew 6:9). The presence of God was not only in the tabernacle, dwelling with Israel, but also His presence was manifested in the cloud during the day and the pillar of fire by night (Exodus 13:21–22; 40:34–36). God's presence was always there, guiding Israel's journey to the Promised Land. Paul certainly had this in mind when he wrote in Romans 8:14, "For as many as are led by the Spirit of God are sons of God." Where Israel was led by the presence of God in the cloud and fire so the disciple today is led by His indwelling Spirit.

---

[40] "Hear, O Israel: the Lord our God, the Lord is one. You shall love the Lord your God with all your heart and with all your soul and with all your being. And these words that I command you today shall be on your heart" (Deuteronomy 6:4–6 ESV).

THE PROMISED LAND

God's presence and leadership did not stop when Israel crossed the Jordan and entered Canaan, the land promised first to Abraham and his descendants and later to Israel. His promise has always been, "I'll be with you" (Deuteronomy 31:23, Joshua 1:6), a promise reiterated by Jesus in Matthew 28:20. The condition or stipulation was that Israel keep "all the words of the law" (Joshua 1:8–9). The necessity of this is obvious when we see Israel's task as reflecting the image of God in the Promised Land. What would be the point of the Promised Land?

Actually the Promised Land is another way of saying "Eden," a land of delight. Notice the descriptions in Exodus 38:8, 17; Numbers 13:17–24; 16:13–14.

For this to be a reality, evil must be purged from the land as leaven was purged from the Passover meal in preparation for freedom from slavery. Apparently, this is the reason behind God going before Israel to drive out the occupants of Canaan, who did not recognize God as the Almighty Creator and Lord of all the earth. The renewing of the covenant was, therefore, essential for this to materialize. For the land to be an appreciated gift from God to Israel, obedience to the laws of God was necessary. Rather than obedience being an arbitrary duty, it was to show gratitude for what God had done on their behalf and also for Israel to have the character (the image of God) befitting inhabitants in Eden, the land of delight or Canaan. Remember: God was the real conqueror. He was the One driving out evil throughout the land through chosen servants. He was the One who was driving evil from the land. When He was obeyed, the conquest was successful. When He was disobeyed, disaster followed. How many times must He repeat this to His created ones?

This was the pattern of deliverance not only during the conquest of Canaan but also four centuries later during the days of the fifteen judges whom God chose as deliverers. Actually, this sequence of events formed the history of the Israelites. Rather than being God's chosen instrument to reflect His image, as the covenant stipulated, and remove evil, Israel became part of the problem[41] (Judges 2:1–3; 11–23).

Time and again, Israel broke the covenant they had made with God while, with unbelievable patience

---

[41] "For your part, you were not to make any covenants with the people living in this land; instead, you were to destroy their altars. Why, then, have you disobeyed my command? Since you have done this, I will no longer drive out the people living in your land. They will be thorns in your sides, and their gods will be a constant temptation to you" (Judges 2:2–3 ESV).

and love for His creation (the whole cosmos Romans 8:18–25), God always kept His part of the covenant (Joshua 24:1–27). The principle never varies. Love the Lord with grateful obedience, and He blesses abundantly. Disobey and evil will destroy the practitioner (Joshua 23:15–16). Of course, this always involves caring for God's gift of land, the earth, by being good stewards (Genesis 1:26–30; 2:15; Joshua 23:15–16). Perhaps we have reversed the usual and erroneous idea about the Lord God destroying the earth when it is humanity who has abandoned its role and is therefore the real culprit.

With a godly couple, Elkana and Hanna, praying fervently for a child, the focus of the biblical narrative changes. However, the biblical principles established thus far do not change. God, with a heavy heart, is still intervening in human affairs to redeem His creation from evil and renew it according to His vision in the beginning; that is, to have His creation reflect His image. The principle of blessing and cursing remain as they are to this day. The covenant is intact, but with one partner, Israel, in violation and God remaining faithful to His part of the covenant. The gift of land remains for the moment, even though the image bearer and caretaker, Israel, has failed in responsibility, forsaken the image of God. Yet the love of God hasn't diminished. What a gracious and merciful God!

The activity of righteous Elkana and the prayer of pious Hanna prevailed. God granted a son, Samuel, who became a shining light amid the dark history of Israel. This amazing intervention of God had happened before with Abraham and Sarah. He would surprise humanity centuries later with a similar event by another righteous couple,

Zachariah and Elizabeth, who became parents of John the Baptist. The purpose of God for His creation would be consummated in spite of the failure of His created ones.

ISRAEL ASKS FOR A KING

But Israel did not adhere to Samuel's attempt to have them rely only on God's powerful and loving presence. They looked at neighboring nations around them with vain eyes and asked for a king. Didn't they already have a king whose name was YHWH? Samuel was distraught because Israel had rejected His appeal. But God said, "They haven't rejected you, Samuel; they have rejected me. Let them have their way but tell them what to expect" (1 Samuel 8:7–9). You wonder what God is up to. How does this fit in His plan to redeem and renew His creation?

God had Samuel anoint a handsome young man named Saul to be Israel's king. His beginning seemed to go well. However, soon he too began to be filled with pride and greed. Israel began to fail to reflect the characteristics of a godly nation. So God intervened again by empowering a young man named David to deliver Israel from a foreign nation. Notice the marvel of God's ways as Samuel anoints David to be king in much the same way that, centuries later, another child of a couple praying for a son, Zachariah and Elizabeth, had a child named John, who anointed Jesus, another king who would deliver God's creation from evil. It will be the jubilee of all jubilees (Leviticus 25:8–22)! David was not always true to his responsibility of reflecting God's image chosen as a shepherd king over God's people. He committed adultery with a beautiful woman named Bathsheba. David also took a census of the people when he went to war suggesting his trust in numbers rather than God. (2 Samuel 24) He also had attributes that did reflect the image of God. His repentance in Psalm 51[42] speaks eloquently of his sorrow for not having a right heart, manifested in his sin with Bathsheba. His staunch desire to attribute successes to God's intervention, not merely for his own ability, surely is a model for all to follow. Yet, Israel's failure to embrace God's will during the conquest, as well as not completely removing foreign gods from the land, continued to be a curse to his reign (Exodus 33:1–2).

David's advice to his son Solomon should serve as a model for fathers of all time.[43] The key to Solomon's

---

[42] "Have mercy on me, O God, according to your unfailing love; according to your great compassion blot out my transgressions. Wash away my all my iniquity and cleanse me from my sin" (Psalm 51:1–2 NIV). The entire psalm is important.

[43] "Keep the charge of the Lord your God, walk in His ways, keep His statutes, His commandments, His precepts, and His testimonies, as it is written in the Law of Moses, that you may do wisely and prosper in all that you do and wherever you turn" (1 Kings 2:3 AB)

success was the desire of his heart as expressed in 1 Kings 3:9.[44] These characteristics explain why the golden years of Israel existed during the reign of David and Solomon.

The premise of blessings and curses, however, are still clearly revealed. Following the ways of God by reflecting His image will result in blessings. Following our own ways and disobeying the purposes for which we were created will result in curses. When Solomon followed the desire expressed in 1 Kings 3:8–9, Israel prospered. When in his later life he neglected teaching his sons and also became entangled with foreign wives, the kingdom began to disintegrate. The kingdom of Israel would never be the same. Foreign

---

[44] "Give me an understanding mind so that I can govern your people well and know the difference between right and wrong. For who by himself is able to govern this great nation of yours?" (NLT)

governments no longer feared Israel because they had left the Lord God.

But God's amazing patience and love for His chosen people, resulted in prophets courageously trying to call Israel back to their covenant with God. God continued to call. He continued to intervene in the affairs of His creation. However, Israel continued to defect from their part of the covenant. To Solomon's credit, he attributed Israel's success to God.[45] Out of gratitude, he built an elaborate edifice to symbolize the presence of God in the land. This became the place where prayers were offered, sacrifices were made, and feasts were held. The temple became one place where heaven and earth merged to acknowledge the power and

---

[45] "You know that my father, David, was not able to build a Temple to honor the name of the Lord his God because of the many wars he waged with surrounding nations. He could not build until the Lord gave him victory over all his enemies. But now the Lord my God has given me peace on every side, and I have no enemies and all is well" (1 Kings 5:3–4 NLT)

glory of the Lord God. There Israel manifested gratitude for the grace and mercy of God.

Worship in the temple had sabbatical overtones. Just as the creation was completed in seven days, so Israel gathered in the temple on the Sabbath to worship the God of creation. Deuteronomy 5:15[46] presents a second facet to temple worship that reminds Israel of the deliverance and freedom from slavery in Egypt. It was nothing short of a merger of heaven and earth!

The merger of heaven and earth became more explicit when the new age began. Christ on the cross pronounced, "It is finished." What was finished? The new creation promised over and over again

---

[46] "You shall remember that you were a slave in the land of Egypt, and the Lord your God brought you out from there by a mighty hand and an outstretched arm; therefore the Lord your God commanded you to observe the Sabbath day." (ESV)

in the narrative about God and His vision for His creation that evil had defaced. In other words, the words of Christ meant that the new creation was completed, the great enemy of death defeated, so we should celebrate by worshiping the Creator with a Sabbath rest as God did when He completed His creation.[47] So the early Christians assembled on the first day of the week,[48] which literally translated is "on the first of the Sabbaths" (*mia ton sabbaton*). This acknowledges that the new age or new creation began at the resurrection of Jesus. Is this pertinent to the rest mentioned in Hebrews 4? This certainly has sabbatical overtones by remembering the past but also looking forward to the return of Christ when the new age will be fully consummated. As Paul averred in 1 Corinthians 11:26, "We celebrate Christ's death until He comes." Worship on the

---

[47] Genesis 2:1–2 (AB)
[48] Acts 20:7 (NIV)

first day of the week or first of Sabbaths gives a foretaste of the restoration of God's creation and anticipates the final completion of God's kingdom on earth as in heaven. This is the true reality of one of the events taking place when Christ returns to earth a second time.

As history rolled on, when Israel adhered to God's leadership with kings such as Josiah, Hezekiah, and Uzziah, they prospered and were blessed. When they rejected God's presence with kings such as Jeroboam, Ahaz, Ahab, and Manessah, disaster followed. This has always been and continues to be the principle of all nations who have graced the earth by God's mercy. Finally, after God's people ignored His discipline decade after decade, God began to use Israel's enemies like Sennacherib and Nebuchadnezzar as instruments to accomplish His purpose of renewal. Actually, the significance of this is that the Kingdom of God on earth has vanished until the true King, Christ, appears on earth and announces that the Kingdom of God is at hand. The point is, just as in Genesis 3 when God removed Adam and Eve from the land of delight, so now God is removing Israel from the land flowing with milk and honey, or Eden. Disobedience has severe consequences. The real tragedy is that this means that the reconciliation of God and humanity is lost.

The astonishing thing is that God's everlasting covenant made with Abraham and renewed with Israel and then with David continued by the grace of God. God's promises were sure in spite of Israel's failure. Time and time again, God sent His spokespeople, prophets, to call Israel back to their purpose of reflecting God's image. During the kingship of Ahab, the king of Israel who did evil in the sight of God, and Jehoshaphat, the king of Judah who tried to recall them to honor God, a new sort of discipline from God became evident. Not only did God's chosen people have to war against the inhabitants of Canaan because they did not obey God and drive them out, but also now they had to contend with neighboring nations such as Egypt, Assyria, and Babylon. To make things worse, Israel and Judah began to fight each other, brother against brother. This is what happens when the kingship of God is forsaken, and the covenant violated.

However, God remained steadfast to His promise to David. Prophets were sent to remind Israel of their covenant with God. The prophets exhorted Israel to return to God with their hearts so His image could be reflected. They constantly reminded Israel and Judah of the consequences of disobedience. For instance, the eight century

B.C. Isaiah told Israel that since they had spurned the love of God, the gift of land would become desolate (Isaiah 1:1–7). Yet there was still hope if they would repent (Isaiah 1:16–20).

The hope of Israel would be in the form of a son from the root of Jesse, the father of David, who would bring a new age where righteousness reigned (Isaiah 11–12).

Another prophet, Hosea, through his heartbreaking experience with an adulterous wife, captured the enormous hurt of God because of Israel's adultery of pursuing other gods.[49] He reminds us that sin against God is much more than breaking a command; it is an actual affront to God that hurts

---

[49] "When Israel was a child, I loved him, and out of Egypt I called my son. But the more I called Israel, the further they went from me. They sacrificed to the Baals and they burned incense to images. It was I who taught Ephraim to walk, taking them by the arms; but they did not realize it was I who healed them" (Hosea 11:1–3 NIV)

deep in God's heart. Thus, Hosea and Isaiah both emphasize the breaking of covenant with God and stress the agonizing consequences.

Amos and Micah, also messengers of God, announced doom for God's people because they did not keep love for God and neighbor as their first priorities. Yet, like Isaiah and Hosea, they foresaw a time when God's love and mercy would trump the foolish disobedience of humanity and recreate a world as He intended in the beginning (Amos 9:11–15; Micah 4:1–13). A marvelous example of the hope they portrayed was seen in God's intervention in the life of His people near the end of Judah's existence of self-rule in Palestine. It came in the form of Josiah, an exemplary king in Judah during the days of Jeremiah. Jeremiah was a prophet and priest, of unusual courage and caring for God's people. Jeremiah worked tirelessly during Josiah's last eight years of reign to get Judah back to living righteously and reflecting God's character to nations around them. Idols were torn down, and worship of YHWH was restored. The temple was rebuilt, and the Word of the Lord was heard anew. The Passover and Feast of Unleavened Bread were observed again.

During this time, Jeremiah was reminding and exhorting the people to repent and devote themselves with all their heart to Jehovah and become true caretakers of their God-given land. However, Josiah was killed in a battle with Egypt, and his sons who reigned after him were not faithful. Jeremiah's life became difficult as he continued to tell kings and subjects that their days were short lived. In spite of his chastisement and pronouncement of doom, with a broken heart, he offered words of hope.[50]

---

[50] Jeremiah 23:5–6.

He foresaw a new covenant, different from the present one because the laws of God would be woven into the hearts of men. The laws of God wouldn't simply be an obstacle to get around or break, but the Word and the man would be one! Jeremiah had such faith in the restoration and God's gift of land that he bought a parcel of land, giving evidence that God would return His people to the Promised Land.

Just as in Genesis 11, the people would not listen. So due to the pride and selfish behavior, both Judah and Israel were cast out of the Promised Land (Eden) and suffered alienation from the loving God. This was strikingly similar to the casting out of Adam and Eve from the garden of Eden in Genesis 3. The words of God's spokesman, Jeremiah, rang true. First, Israel was captured and taken to a foreign land, Assyria, to become servants of foreigners.

Then Judah, with Solomon's temple destroyed, was captured and taken to Babylon. The pathetic aspect of these events were that God used foreign rulers to accomplish His will (2 Chronicles 24:24; 23:11; 26:6–11). The Assyrian captives became so absorbed into Assyrian culture that they never were again known as the nation of Israel. Judah would remain servants to foreign rulers until Jerusalem was destroyed by the Romans in AD 66–70. They traded freedom for slavery by rejecting the kingship of God. This is very similar to eating the tree of knowledge of good and evil in the garden of Eden when they could have eaten of the tree of life. They traded their living king for lifeless kings.

Even when God's people were in captivity, the unbelievable resolve of God to have His creation restored to His vision in the beginning is evident. God called another spokesman named Ezekiel to exhort His people to trust YHWH to deliver them from Babylonian captivity. Ezekiel partnered with the visions of God and saw not only a restored temple that suggested the return of God but also a renewal of life. Perhaps the most suggestive of his visions came in chapter 37 where Ezekiel saw dry bones come to life, fulfilling the vision in chapter 36 where Israel would again be given a heart with a spirit within to cause them to walk with God. These visions were followed with the most revealing vision about God's intent to renew His creation from death to life. The Dead Sea would have such abundance of life that fishermen would line its banks (chapter 47). If a vision such as this doesn't stimulate hope in the love, mercy, and justice of God, what will? Couple that with Jeremiah's great statement in Jeremiah 31[51] and you have a classic view of God's intent to recreate new heavens and a new earth where righteousness is the prevailing culture.

And just when you think it couldn't get any better, it does with the message of the sixth century Isaiah. Isaiah's message was a classic message of trust in God for a new creation of the heavens and earth (chapters 65–66). This provocative message was introduced with words comforting the captives in Babylonia (Isaiah 40:1–11). This comfort was based on two very important principles. First, a gracious God had erased the sinful acts of the

---

[51] "Behold, the days are coming, declares the Lord, when I will make a new covenant with the house of Israel and with the house of Judah, not like the covenant I made with their fathers on the day when I took them by the hand to bring them out of the land of Egypt, my covenant which they broke, though I was their husband, declares the Lord. But this is the covenant I will make with the house of Israel after those days, declares the Lord: I will put my law within them, and I will write it on their hearts. And I will be their God and they shall be my people" (Jeremiah 31:31–33 ESV)

past. Second, He had, because of this forgiveness, reconciled Israel to Himself. This was God's doing and His alone. It was not based on Israel's good deeds. However, righteous deeds must have been performed out of sheer gratitude for the grace and mercy of an unbelievable God. The most obvious act of appreciation was a humble heart and a servant disposition.

Among the contrasts of these prophecies with earlier prophets is that they gave no specifics. That is, the prophet wasn't named, nor was the location or time of the prophecies given. The prophecies were not specified for God's people in Babylon, Assyria, Palestine, or Egypt.[52] They apparently were meant for God-fearing people everywhere. This might explain one reason why Isaiah was the

---

[52] "But you, O Israel, my servant, Jacob, whom I have chosen, you descendants of Abraham my friend. I took you from the ends of the earth, from its farthest corners I called you" (NIV).

prophet most often quoted in the New Covenant. He humorously asked God's people to examine the power of their gods with the power of YHWH and then decide who they would follow (chapters 40–41:29).

Isaiah boldly stated that God had chosen His people to be servants.[53] This referred first to Israel and then to Jesus and finally to followers of Jesus. Paul concurred centuries later.[54] Isaiah insisted that through being a servant, Israel would reflect the image of God and be a light to the nations around them. This was one of the first, but not

---

[53] "Behold my servant, whom I uphold, my chosen, in whom my soul delights; I have put my Spirit upon him; he will bring forth justice to the nations. He will not cry aloud or life up his voice, or make it heard in the street; a bruised reed he will not break, and a faintly burning wick he will not quench, he will faithfully bring forth justice. He will not grow faint or be discouraged till he has established justice in the earth, and the coastlands wait for his law" (Isaiah 42:1–4 ESV).

[54] "Blessed be the God and Father of our Lord Jesus Christ, who has blessed us with every spiritual blessing in the heavenly places in Christ, just as He chose us in Him before the foundations of the world that we would be holy and blameless before Him" (Ephesians 1:3–4 NESB).

the only, mention that God's intent was to have all humanity who believe in Him to honor and follow His will. The plot of the biblical narrative began to widen to encompass the entire world, not just Israel, that being all who honored Him as Creator and Lord over creation. Also, it had ramifications for land when God would create new heavens and earth (Isaiah 65, 66). This was necessary for the completion of the new age because, through sin the land had been cursed (Genesis 3:17). That was one reason Paul wrote in Romans 8:18–25,

> I consider that our present sufferings are not worth comparing with the glory that will be revealed in us. The creation waits in eager expectation for the sons of God to be revealed. For the creation was subjected to frustration, not by its own choice, but by the will of the one who subjected it, in hope

that the creation itself will be liberated from its bondage to decay and brought into the glorious freedom of the children of God. We know that the whole creation has been groaning as in the pains of childbirth right up to the present time. Not only so, but we ourselves, who have the first fruits of the Spirit, groan inwardly as we wait eagerly for our adoption as sons, the redemption of our bodies. For in this hope we were saved. But hope that is seen is not hope at all. Who hopes for what he already has? But if we hope for what we do not yet have, we wait for it patiently.

When the new earth is created, God's vision in Genesis 1–2 will be consummated. This explains, in part, the significance of Jesus' last words in Matthew 28:18–20! When God pushed back the water and dry land appeared, He called it "earth" (Genesis 1:10). When God created humanity, He identified humankind with earth (Genesis 2:7) as if to say, "This is your home I have given you."[55] Earth became a place of delight or Eden (Genesis 2:8). When the new earth is created, it too will be a place of delight for the redeemed ones. The prevailing culture will be a place where righteousness dwells. But more about this later.

Isaiah was right on when he said in Isaiah 54:10, speaking for God, "Though the mountains depart and the hills be shaken, yet my love shall not depart from my chosen ones, nor shall my covenant of peace be removed."

---

[55] "May you be blessed by the Lord, who made heaven and earth. The heavens belong to the Lord, but he has given the earth to all humanity" (Psalm 115:15–16 NLT).

ISRAEL IN EXILE

As 2 Chronicles states in chapter 36:21–23, Cyrus, commander of Persia, through the provision of God, decreed that the captives were free to return to the Promised Land. More specifically and telling, the seventy years in captivity had sabbatical overtones. The "rest" referred to surely had Genesis 2:2 in mind; that is, the rest of God after the creation. The emphasis is as it has always been, God is doing a new thing (Isaiah 43:19). His people can begin anew to be the people He chose to reflect His image to the nations around them (Isaiah 42:6; 49:6). Also, according to Deuteronomy 5:14–15, the Sabbath reminded Israel of the freedom from slavery that God gave them. The implication is obvious. All of this, creation, land, rest, and freedom, is implied by the choice of seventy (Sabbath) years of captivity and then freedom to return to the Promised Land to be true caretakers.

With the decree of Cyrus in hand, Zerubbabel and Jeshua led the first group of Israelites back to Jerusalem and laid the foundation for the second temple. While it gave a reason for joyful celebration, many of the old men who lived during the days of Solomon's temple wept because it did not compare to the splendor of the first temple.[56]

However, the adversaries living in Judah, and elsewhere had the building project stopped until Darius became king of Persia. With the help of two notable prophets, Haggai and Zechariah, the building resumed and was completed in the twelfth month of the sixth year of Darius' reign.

[56] "But many of the older priests and Levites and family heads, who had seen the former temple, wept aloud when they saw the foundation of this temple being laid" (Ezra 3:12 NIV).

After another sixty years passed, Ezra the scribe, learned in the law, also came and read the law in the hearing of the people. But all was not well. The people still had not removed foreigners from the land. In fact, many had married foreign women, forsaking the command of God not to do so. This indicated the problem Jeremiah warned about, which was that many in Israel had not allowed the law to be written on their hearts. It was what the serpent suggested in Genesis 3. The law was something that could be circumvented.

A hundred years after the first Israelites returned to Jerusalem, Nehemiah was commanded by Artaxerxes, the king of Persia, to repair the walls of Jerusalem. Nehemiah also asked Israel to repent for breaking the covenant they had made with God. Gathering the priest, Levites, singers, and others, Nehemiah asked them to renew their covenant and make a vow to keep the law. This, they did. It seemed that the glory days of old had returned. But, alas, not quite! Israel was still under foreign rule, a reminder of what Samuel had warned about centuries earlier. It gets worse. Malachi the prophet said that the people began to rob God by sacrificing inferior animals and not tithing properly. Even the priests became corrupt. So it appeared that God withdrew His spokespeople again. His word, copied by the scribes, was sufficient. But God's steadfast love for His people, as well as His vision for His creation, never ceased. What a God!

GREEK DOMINATION

The Greeks came and, under the brilliance of Alexander, became dominant in the world. Alexander brought Greek culture, including the Greek language, wherever he conquered. Hebrew manuscripts were, of necessity, translated into the Greek language. This became known as the Septuagint (a Latin word for seventy sometimes referred to with the Roman numerals LXX) because it was done by seventy scholars in Alexandria, Africa, a city named after the conqueror. At his untimely death, most of the conquered land was divided among his generals, namely Ptolemy and Seleucus. Judah, after many wars, finally came under the rule of the Seleucids. The Seleucid dynasty were strong adherents to Hellenizing the land they controlled. They built a gymnasium near the temple where Gentiles played games, primarily in the nude. The Jewish youth tried in vain to hide their circumcision. Seleucus IV even had the image of a pig placed in the temple and forbade the Jewish people from worshiping on the Sabbath. Finally, a God-worshiping family, the Maccabees, had had enough and revolted, causing more bitter conflicts.

ROMAN DOMINATION

The Romans were growing stronger and finally conquered the God-given land of the Israelites. After much conniving, the crafty Herod became king over most of the Promised Land. This has been, of necessity, a very brief and perhaps unsatisfying history of a long chain of events involving God's chosen people. But details would take us too far afield for the purpose of this writing. The reader is referred to *The New Testament Era* by Bo Reicke; the writings of Josephus; and the apocryphal books of the Maccabees and Esdras for a complete detailed discussion of events during the four centuries before the new covenant begins.

THE NEW COVENANT

The new covenant begins, as described by Paul in Galatians 4:4–5, "But when the time had fully come, God sent His Son, born of a woman, born under the law, to redeem those under the law, that we might receive the full rights of sons." This began an era in history that words are inadequate to describe. With the birth, life, death and resurrection of Jesus, the Son of God, a new relationship between God and His chosen people began. In short, the long promised new age was here now and will be consummated when He returns. The longstanding promises of God had become actual. He had returned to Zion, the Promised Land. The reality of that was sung by the heavenly host at his birth, "Peace on earth and goodwill to man." That too suggested a promise of God to be fulfilled after He returns a second time.

God was doing a new thing. Since Israel had failed to be the light of the world and instead became part of the problem, God Himself did what Israel had failed to do by coming in the form of a person in the flesh to be the light for the nations (John 1:9; 8:12; 9:5). The promise in Malachi 3:1 of God returning to Zion was fulfilled. The faithfulness of God has materialized before the eyes of the world. The king with His promised kingdom has arrived (Matthew 4:23; Mark 1:15; Luke 11:20)! The kingdom has come and will be fully consummated when the Christ (King) returns.

For the first time since Genesis 2 when God walked in the garden He created, in Jesus, He walks again in His garden. Heaven and earth have merged to be the dwelling of both God and humankind.[57] Matthew presented this in his narrative about the *magoi* coming from the east. It is significant that the word *magoi* is a Persian word meaning "someone with exceptional wisdom." Where did they get such wisdom? According to Proverbs 2:6, true wisdom comes only from God, who is wisdom. Bible readers are familiar with God visiting in special events through messengers. Also, notice that this is a fulfillment of a prophecy in Isaiah 42:6[58] about giving light to Gentiles. God chose Israel to be the light of the world, but they failed. Now God was doing Himself what Israel failed to do. Luke further described the merging of heaven

---

[57] "And this is His plan: At the right time He will bring everything together under the authority of Christ—everything in heaven and on earth" (Ephesians 1:10 NLT).

[58] "I am The Lord, I have called you in righteousness, I will also hold you by the hand and watch over you, and I will appoint you as a covenant to the people, as a light to the nations." (NASB)

and earth through Jesus' birth by indicating that the heavenly host rejoiced and sang, "Glory to God in the highest heaven, and peace on earth to all whom God favors" (Luke 2:13–14). Shepherds were also keeping watch. Yes, shepherds and angels, heaven and earth, rejoicing at the birth of the King. Yes, His name shall be called Jesus because He will save people from their sin. This should not be thought of as some narcissistic idea that salvation is only about me. Rather, it means that through Jesus, obedient humanity will be reconciled to God.

The four gospels of Matthew, Mark, Luke, and John are our primary sources to comprehend the meaning of Jesus. First, the word "gospel" (*euangellion*) means "good news." That is, the gospels are not presenting theories or myths; the good news is an actual event. Something happened! In this case, the event that happened was very good.

The synoptic gospels, Matthew, Mark, and Luke, introduce their story by saying that one of the first statements Jesus made to explain why He came was, "Repent for the Kingdom of God (heaven) is arriving" (Matthew 4:17; Mark 1:15; Luke 4:43). Israel had rejected God as their king, with few exceptions, since the days of Samuel (1 Samuel 8). Now, through Jesus Christ (Jesus is His name; Christ is His title), the kingdom is being restored on earth as it is in heaven. That is good news in itself, but there is more. John's story has a parallel but different emphasis. He begins with the creation story, "In the beginning" (Genesis 1:1; John 1:1). His story reaches a climax when Jesus on the cross says, "It is finished" (John 19:30). These words are so similar to the words in Genesis 2:1 when the creation story ended that the intent is obvious. The new creation is finished! John's story is about Jesus accomplishing a new creation or a new era. The new creation that He began will not be fully consummated until He returns. The first century Jews, under Roman control, were eagerly waiting for God to return as He had promised through the prophets.[59] However, Jesus did not come as the conquering emperor that they wanted, so most of them, sadly, rejected Him.

The four gospels tell the same story but from different perspectives. Matthew begins his narrative with a genealogy. The genealogy, in graphic detail, explains how Israel's rather sordid history of disobedience led them into exile,

---

[59] "Rejoice greatly, O daughter of Zion! Shout, Daughter of Jerusalem! See, your King comes to you, righteous and having salvation ..." (Zechariah 9:9 NIV) "See, I will send my messenger, who will prepare the way before me. Then suddenly the Lord you are seeking will come to His temple" (Malachi 3:1 NIV).

estrangement from God. This is Genesis 3 all over again, where Adam and Eve were cast out of the garden, which, in essence, meant alienation from God. The genealogy then climaxes with the birth of Jesus who takes sin, which is the cause of estrangement, away and, by doing so, reconciles people with God. Only a true king can do this for his subjects.

All of the gospels refer to the Jordan immersions as a signal that the new age has begun (Matt 3:13–14; Mark 1:9–11; Luke 3:21–22; John1:29–33). Several concepts are significant in this event. First, there is a heavy emphasis on the voice from heaven. "This is my Son in whom I love; with Him I am well pleased."[60] This statement is a blending of two biblical themes. One theme comes from Psalm 2 where the psalmist declares that God's

---

[60] Matthew 3:17 (NIV).

Son will rule with a rod of iron—a lion-of-Judah concept (Genesis 49:9). The other biblical theme comes from Isaiah 42 where the servant of the Lord is a delight to God. This references the life of the Lamb of God (John 1:29). Both of these themes are united in the throne scene in Revelation (Revelation 5:5–6). Another concept suggested by immersion in the Jordan is an exodus theme. The Jordan historically was viewed as the boundary between the wilderness and the Promised Land.

When the water was pushed, Israel crossed into the land flowing with milk and honey, or Eden, a land of delight (Exodus 3:8; Deuteronomy 6:3). This not only has freedom themes, such as freeing Israel from Egyptian bondage and taking them to the promised land, but it also has biblical themes of God pushing the water back so dry land could appear. In the Genesis creation story, God pushed the water back, and dry land appeared on which He placed humankind to be caretakers. Part of the exodus story is about God parting the water of the Red Sea so Israel could pass safely from the Egyptians. Forty years later, Israel crossed the river Jordan on dry land into Palestine to be God's caretakers and a light to the Gentiles there. God pushing the water back has enormous ramifications. The Revelation letter states that the evil beast came from the water representing the source of evil (Revelation 13:1–8). Also, Revelation states that when Christ returns, "The sea will be no more," suggesting that evil will be purged from the earth. Obviously, this is what John was alluding to when he wrote, "Behold the lamb of God who takes away the sin of the world" (John 1:29).

Jesus' conversation with Nicodemus in John 3 is revealing. To participate or live in the new age, he must be born again. That birth is spoken of in John 3:5–6. Later, Paul would say the same thing in 2 Corinthians 5:17 but in a different context: "Therefore, if any person is in Christ he is a new creation. The old has passed away. Behold, the new has come."[61]

Much of the teaching of Jesus pertains to the lifestyle of the new humankind living in the new age. It is interesting as well as significant that Matthew has Jesus on a mountain as He begins to teach in chapter 5. Certainly, he wants the reader to think of another mountain, Mount Sinai, where God gave Moses conduct principles (Exodus 20). Those words were the open door to the heart of God. There are both similarities and dissimilarities between the two teachings on the mountain. Both espouse humility and reverence before God. Both advocate loving God and neighbor. There

---

[61] (AB)

are other important similarities, but these will get us on the right track to understand the meaning. The dissimilarities are provocative. For instance, the Mount Sinai teaching has the element of compliance. The teaching of Jesus, however, has more emphasis on the prophecy of Jeremiah in chapter 31 of his book. In other words, the teaching of Jesus emphasizes practicing the image or likeness of God not just to comply but because that's what life in the new age entails. It personifies the prayer of David in Psalm 51, "Lord don't cast me away from your presence but cleanse me and give me a new heart and a right spirit" (Psalm 51:7, 10).

Let's look at this practically. For instance, the man living life in the new age doesn't say, "Well, I haven't actually committed adultery with another woman, so I've passed the test." Now as a citizen of the new age and a member of the kingdom of God, the teaching is, "Whoever looks at a woman lustfully has already committed adultery in his heart" (Matthew 5:28). Jesus has proclaimed a totally new standard. However, He has described the new people living in the new age. Paul describes this as being a new creation.[62] John expresses essentially the same thought in 1 John 3:15, "Whoever is angry with his brother is a murderer in his heart." The emphasis goes far beyond mere compliance. Rather, the emphasis is on who we are as newly created people. The immersed person is created to reflect the image of God and be a true caretaker in His wonderful garden of delight. This is the world, earth, He has made for us.[63] Yet heaven and earth belong to the Lord[64] (Psalm 89:11).

---

[62] "Therefore, if anyone is in Christ, he is a new creation. The old has passed away; behold, the new has come." (2 Corinthians 5:17 NIV)

[63] "The heavens are the Lord's heavens, but the earth he has given to the children of man" (Psalm 115:16 NLT).

[64] "The heavens are yours; the earth also is yours; the world and all that is in it, you have founded them" (Psalm 89:11 NLT).

Is it really possible to live according to the standards Jesus is suggesting—a life without lust, anger, and many other human weaknesses? Humanly speaking, this is impossible, but with God all things are possible. John in his first epistle is insightful when he says that when the person who walks in the light as Jesus is in the light, His blood (life) cleanses us from all sin (1 John 1:7). The word he uses is *katharos*, a present active indicative verb that suggests a constant cleansing as we walk in the footsteps of Jesus. He fleshes the concept out in chapter 2. Here he refers to the idea of the mercy seat in the tabernacle. Specifically, he writes, "If we sin we have an advocate (*paraklaton*—one who stands beside us) Jesus Christ, the righteous who is the propitiation of our sins" (chapter 2:1–2). The word he wrote for propitiation is *hilasmos*, "a covering." This word is a Greek translation for the Hebrew word *kapporet*, meaning "mercy seat," as in the tabernacle (Leviticus 16:14–15). In other words, those who are in Christ (Galatians 3:27) and are walking as Jesus walked, God sees them through the covering of Jesus Christ who is our mercy seat. Just as the mercy seat covered Israel's covenant with God, so Jesus covers our covenant with God. These are those of whom Paul spoke in (Colossians 1:12; Ephesians 1:3–4) who are the heirs of God's gifts.

Another form of Jesus' teaching is parables. Contrary to common belief, the parables are not like Aesop's fables with a nice little moral. They are mostly about Israel's history and their relationship with God. They tell of both Israel's failures and successes. For instance, the parable about the father with two sons in Luke 15 has a backdrop of Israel's faraway captivity in Babylon and their return as pictured in Ezra and Nehemiah.

In fact, the parable is more about a giving, hurting, forgiving father than about a prodigal son and elder brother. The parable relates how God, the Father, gave Israel, His children, the Promised Land, only to watch them reject and misuse His gift. You can feel His hurt as Israel mistreats and finally loses the gift and goes far away in exile. But through the marvelous intervention of God, they finally return home to Palestine, only to have their brothers there complain of their return and try to hinder building the temple and its wall. There are other similar parables, such as the seed and sower in Mark 4 or the parable of the wicked tenants in Matthew 21 who rejected God's messengers and finally killed His Son. They are graphic descriptions of Israel's historic relationship with God.

The miracles present another similar but dissimilar teaching. They are not only about the healing power of Jesus but also about a foretaste of life without sin that God had in mind during the creation in Genesis and, later, the new creation that will be fully realized when the Christ returns. Remember: sin, disease, affliction, and even death are the results of sin.[65] When the kingdom of God comes in its fullness on earth with the return of the King, Jesus Christ, and the earth has been purged of evil, diseases will be no more.[66] By miracles, Jesus is graphically demonstrating that the kingdom of God has come, and the prospect of renewed life is possible.

---

[65] "But so that you may know that the Son of Man has authority on earth to forgive sin—then He said to the paralytic, Get up, pick up your bed and go home" (Matthew 9:6 NASB)

[66] "I heard a shout from the throne, saying, look, the home of God is now among his people! He will live with them, and they will be his people, God himself will be with them. He will remove all of their sorrows, and there will be no more death or sorrow or crying or pain. For the old world and its evils are gone forever" (Revelation 21:3–4 NLT).

So what were the teachings, miracles, and the Word becoming flesh all about? He was inaugurating His kingdom on earth as the first words the gospels have Him affirm. Peter, and others, finally understood when He asked them, "Who do *you* say I am?" (Matthew 16:15–19). Peter's response is revealing. "You are the King, the Son of the living God." Yes, this is the verdict when the teachings, miracles, and Jesus' entire activities are put into perspective. But, alas, the prophecy from Isaiah[67] repeated by Jesus in Mark 4:12 is embodied by multitudes who reject Jesus as the Christ. Throughout His life, the Christ (King) constantly spoke about the kingdom of God. It is important to note that the kingdom of God is not a democracy, socialism, or communism. It is a theocracy with Jesus as its King until He turns

---

[67] "And he said, "Go. And say to this people; Keep on hearing, but do not understand; keep on seeing, but do not perceive" (Isaiah 6:9 (ESV).

it back to the Father as it was before the days of Samuel (1 Samuel 8:5–7; 1 Corinthians 15:24).

However, in spite of Jesus' teachings, miracles, and deeds performed to demonstrate the true meaning of the law, the religious leaders not only rejected Him but stirred up the multitudes to betray Him. Their false accusations against Him demonstrate how easy scripture can be misconstrued for selfish purposes. For instance, when they accused Jesus of claiming to be the Son of God, they quoted Leviticus 24:16 as a reason that He should die for blaspheming. This didn't work, so they then tried another tactic to get the Romans to crucify Jesus. "He claimed to be a king," they said (John 19:12). This cinched Jesus' crucifixion because the Romans did not tolerate any competition with Caesar. Jesus then was crucified by both the leading Jews and the Romans. The interesting truth is that there is another element here that belies the hidden truth. The Jewish leaders admitted that they had no other king except Caesar (John 19:15).

Another important episode in the trial of Jesus was a tradition that the Romans would release one person the Jews requested during the Passover festival. The Jews requested the release of Barabbas, a criminal accused of sedition and murder. This indicates that we are like Barabbas, the guilty going free, while Jesus, the Savior, is crucified in our place! Passover, from its beginning in Exodus 12, has signified freedom or a "passing over" because of the blood of the lamb. No wonder Paul says that Jesus is our Passover Lamb (1 Corinthians 5:7). Grace, grace, God's grace, grace greater than our sins!

Chronology of the crucifixion events is significant to all four of the gospel writers. For instance, all four gospels refer to the Passover meal. The implication being that not only was Jesus the reality of the Passover lamb in Exodus 12 but also a new covenant was realized. This means, as the blood of the lamb was put on the Israelite houses to spare those inside, now the blood of Jesus spares the life of those who believe He was the Christ. Paul stated it well when he wrote to the Corinthians, "Christ our Passover lamb has been sacrificed" (1 Corinthians 5:7). The new covenant between the follower of Christ and God is also affirmed. This covenant is based upon the believer casting out the leaven that corrupts human life (1 Corinthians 5:8). Notice the prevailing idea of purging or cleansing (katharos the Greek word from which we get the English word cauterize). This makes it possible for the cleansed person to reflect the image of God as he or she was created to do. According to Isaiah 59:1–2,[68] it is sin, or disobedience, that separates a person from God.

All four gospels allude to the time of day Jesus was crucified. They are surely making reference to the time of day when the sacrificial lamb was killed in the temple. Josephus, a first-century historian, states that the sacrificial lamb was offered during the ninth hour or three in the afternoon.[69] No wonder that when the light of the world died (John 8:12), darkness spread over the land! The light of the world had been crucified because of greed and misunderstanding. The

---

[68] "Behold, the Lord's hand is not so short that he cannot save; nor is His ear so dull that it cannot hear. But your iniquities have made a separation between you and your God, and your sins have hidden His face from you so that He does not hear" (NASB).

[69] "And any one may hence learn how very great piety we exercise towards God, and the observance of His laws, since the priests were not hindered from their sacred ministrations by their fear during this siege, but did still twice a day, in the morning and about the ninth hour, offer their sacrifices on the altar" (Josephus, *Antiquities of the Jews* 14:4:3).

innocent died; the guilty went free. It seemed that evil had won. But things were not what they seemed to be.

When Jesus quoted from Psalm 22, "My God, why have you forsaken me," it sounded almost like defeat. However, when you read the entire Psalm, there is a note of hope and victory. For instance, speaking of the Lord in verse 24, the text says, "He has not despised or disdained the suffering of the afflicted one. He has not hidden his face from him but has listened to his cry for help." Or again, in verses 27–28, the message of hope and victory ring out, "All the ends of the earth will turn to the Lord, and all the families of the earth will bow down before Him, for dominion belongs to the Lord, and He rules over the nations."

Jesus knew that the faithful of Israel knew this psalm from beginning to end. He was calling attention, not to despair, but to hope and victory.

Jesus was crucified and placed in a tomb in a garden. In Genesis 3, the garden story of life was turned into disobedience and death. By contrast, in this garden, death was turned into life as the power of God was revealed in the resurrection of Jesus. Most translations translate John 20:1, as well as Acts 20:7, "on the first day of the week." However, a literal translation of the Greek text, mia ton sabbaton, is "on the first of the Sabbaths." This phrase is rich and full of ramifications. It certainly alludes to the creation narrative in Genesis when God rested on the seventh (Sabbath) day after the creation was finished. Notice that on the cross Jesus uttered, "It is finished," and rested on the Sabbath day. Overtones of the new creation are everywhere in the crucifixion and resurrection events. Also, there are important ties to the Hebrew writing about entering into His rest. The promise of resting as He did is still a sure promise, so be alert and do not come short of it. We have had the good news spoken to us just like they did. However, since they rejected the message, it was of no value to them. The reason is they did not obey it with trust. So God said, "They shall not enter my rest."[70]Now when we believe and obey we have access to that rest, just like God said, "So then there remains a Sabbath rest for the people of God."[71]

The implication obviously is the new creation is completed. That briefly sums up the life of Christ. That's why He came! The resurrection of Christ on the first of the Sabbaths signals the reality for

---

[70] Hebrews 4:5 (NLT)
[71] Hebrews 4:9 (NLT)

124

everyone. So when Christians gather to participate in the unleavened bread (His body that is the temple of God where sin is no more) and the cup (the blood or life of Christ that covers the participant's sin), they are announcing to the world their belief in the resurrection of Jesus. This affirms the new creation is here. The newly created people (1 Corinthians 5:17) are celebrating the new creation. Through the purging of leaven from God's people, heaven and earth are merged together again, fulfilling God's vision in the beginning.

It was on this mia ton sabbaton that Peter and John ran to the tomb to check out Mary's statement that the body of Jesus was missing from the tomb. The Greek manuscripts describing this incident in John's gospel are much more revealing than most English translations. The English versions use the same word to describe Peter and John entering the tomb:

"They saw." However, the Greek manuscripts use different words to describe what they saw when they entered the tomb. When Peter "saw," the original manuscript uses the word *blepo*, meaning, more or less, a casual look. In contrast, the word used when John "saw" is a different word, *eiden*, whose root is *oraro*, meaning "to observe, scrutinize, or to mark with knowledge." So he believed. This surely refers to statements he had heard Jesus say about His death and resurrection (John 14:1–4). Everything in the tomb was exactly as they had left it when Jesus' body was placed there, the napkin and grave clothes. The only thing missing was the body.

A bodily resurrection cannot be overemphasized. Biblical writings of the gospels as well as Paul clearly state that there were witnesses who saw and recognized a bodily resurrected Jesus (John 20:19–31; 1 Corinthians 15:3–8). This was no mirage, ghost, or mere spirit. They saw their beloved Master in person but with a difference. Paul describes Him as the first fruits of those who have fallen asleep (1 Corinthians 15:20). This suggests that those people who are newly created in His image will have a similar bodily resurrection. They will not be resurrected to some kind of solely spiritual (non-body) existence. The Greek philosophers taught that the life after death would be some sort of spiritual or nonbody existence. They referred to it as the immortality of the soul. But this is totally contrary to biblical teaching.

For instance, in Romans 8:17, Paul clearly states that "creation waits with eager longing for the revealing of the sons of God because creation was subjected to futility and will be free from its bondage to corruption." This seems to suggest bodies with substance. Further, he avers that those who are first fruits of the Spirit await the redemption of their bodies. This suggests that our resurrection will be similar to the bodily resurrection of Jesus. This doesn't sound as though, as some of our songs state, we'll fly away and leave this world because it isn't our home for some sort of immortality of the soul existence, as the Greek philosophers taught.

One of the reasons some Christians hold that view is due to several erroneous interpretations of scripture. One of these is bad theology based on 1 Thessalonians 4:17 where Paul says the resurrected people shall meet the Christ in the air and be with Him always.[72] The word translated air is *aera* and could just as easily mean "atmosphere" or "expanse" as used in Genesis 1 where God called it "sky" or "heaven" (Genesis 1:8). The Bible reader

---

[72] "Then we who are alive and remain will be caught up together with them in the clouds to meet the Lord in the air, and so shall we always be with the Lord" (NASB).

is familiar with the use of clouds referring to the presence of God, as in the wilderness leading Israel by day or the voice from the cloud in the transfiguration narrative that states, "This is my Beloved Son in whom I am well pleased, listen to Him" (Matthew 17:5; Mark 9:7; Luke 9:35). I suggest that 1 Thessalonians 4:13–18 is alluding to an identical theme. Also, refer to the ascension of Jesus in Acts 1:9–11. The terms "up" or "down," though useful, can be misleading. When we say a child goes up a grade in school, we don't mean the child goes to the second story of the building. The child only advances to new experiences. When we say an official in government or a corporation steps down, we are only saying he or she has a new role.

Also, Paul is using a well-known cultural event to demonstrate the idea. Frescos and paintings all through the early and Middle Ages present the idea of crowds meeting soldiers and ushering them into town after their victories. We even have a related biblical example that should help in understanding what Paul had in mind. We call it the triumphal entry into Jerusalem where crowds went out to meet Jesus and usher Him into the city (Matthew 21; Mark 11; Luke 19; John 12). The precedent for this was well established in the history of kings in Israel (2 Kings 9:13). So this is not some spirit going away from this earth to another home. It simply is another way of saying that Jesus and His people will be together forever when the new creation is fully consummated when Christ returns to earth.

With the ascension of Jesus came a promise of His return. If the first return of God, referred to earlier in Malachi, caused the angels to rejoice and sing "peace on earth and goodwill to men," surely His second visit will affect all of creation with rejoicing and singing comparable to the scene in Revelation 4. The promise of His return was spoken by two men in white (Acts 1:10). Perhaps referring to the same two that Mary saw sitting where Jesus had laid in the tomb. This becomes more likely when we translate the Greek word used in John 20:12 (*angelos*) as "messengers" rather than transliterating the word as "angels." Obviously, this is a reference to the two figures on each end of the mercy seat in Exodus 25:18.

THE SECOND VISIT OF JESUS

The second visit of the Son of Man will have deeper and wider ramifications than His first visit, as dynamic as that was. This second visit will be the consummation of God's vision for His entire creation from the beginning. Justice will prevail through the judgment of God. Every knee will bow and confess an acknowledgment of God (Romans 14:11; Philippians 2:10–11). The vision of Isaiah will come to pass with new heavens and a new earth where righteousness saturates all of God's creation. Evil will be no more!

Paul states this clearly in Romans 8:19–23.[73] Notice the two parts of Paul's statement. First, the creation itself will be set free from its bondage to decay, an obvious reference to Genesis 3:17–18 where the land is cursed because of disobedience. Also, in verse 23 of Romans 8, Paul affirms that men who have been born again and are recipients

---

[73] "The creation waits in eager expectation for the sons of God to be revealed. For the creation was subjected to frustration, not by its own choice, but by the will of the one who subjected it, in hope that the creation itself will be liberated from its bondage to decay and brought into the glorious freedom of the children of God. We know that the whole creation has been groaning, as in the pains of child-birth right up to the present time" (NIV).

of the Holy Spirit (Acts 2:38) will be bodily redeemed. This is the new heavens and new earth. Both creation and men have been purged from the effects of evil.

Peter concurs with Paul when he envisioned in 2 Peter 3:10–13 a new heaven and a new earth. He writes about the elements being dissolved with fire and everything on earth exposed. Some interpret this as meaning that the earth disappears. But this is bad theology and contrary to the entire biblical theme. Fire is often spoken of in the Bible as a cleansing agent. I suggest that this is what Peter is referencing (Matthew 3:12; Luke 12:49). Peter is saying that the earth will be purged of its curse just as humanity is purged from sin. The purging is much like the purging from the flood. Therefore,

Peter also looks forward to a new heaven and a new earth (verse 13).[74]

John also writes about the time when evil is purged from all of God's creation.[75] He states that the sea will be no more—not the earth but the sea. He envisions that the sea is where evil comes from.[76] John concludes his amazing vision by speaking of the new heaven and new earth. The reality is beyond description. In Revelation 21 and 22, John paints a word picture that stretches our imaginations. This is what God envisioned when He created the heavens and earth with humanity as His partners and caretakers. For that, we are

---

[74] "But according to his promise we are waiting for new heavens and a new earth in which righteousness dwells"(ESV).

[75] "And I saw the beast and the kings of the earth and their armies assembled to make war against Him who sat on the horse and against His army. And the beast was seized, and with him the false prophet who performed the signs in his presence by which he deceived those who had received the mark of the beast and those who worshiped his image; these two were thrown alive into the lake of fire which burns with brimstone" (Revelation 19:19–20 NASB).

[76] "And I saw a beast coming out of the sea" (Revelation 13:1 NIV).

filled to overflowing with hope. Thank You, Lord, our Father, for being the Holy God of us all! We look forward to living forever with You on Your new beautiful garden of Eden where the heavens and earth will be as You envisioned it in the beginning

CONCLUSIONS

God created the heavens and earth to reflect His glory and majestic power. The climatic creation was man and woman to be His partners in caring for His creation. The diabolos (Devil) deceived the first man and woman into disobeying God.

The biblical narrative explains God's resolve to recreate the heavens and earth, as well as humankind, so that they can again reflect the glory and power of the Creator.

The first eleven chapters of Genesis set the stage for the biblical story. The call of Abraham, in chapter 12, present the specifics of how humanity can partner with God to remediate the problem of evil from God's creation. This is accomplished when humanity, with prayer, obeys the voice of God. Evil, or sin, is a problem that affects both humankind and God. How can humanity reflect God's image when they succumb to sin? How can God's creation be as He intended when His creation, humankind, disobeys.

The resolution, on humanity's behalf, is nothing short of a new creation (2 Corinthians 5:17; John 3:3–8). The solution on God's behalf is the creation of new heavens and earth (Isaiah 65:17; 66:22; 2 Peter 3:13; Revelation 21:1). The remedy will take centuries of God hurting as He watches His creatures struggling, maturing, lost, and then finding their way to obedience and reflecting God's image.

Those who finally acknowledge God with a new heart and obedience are the ones the Bible explains are "those who are chosen before the foundation of the world" (Ephesians 1:4; Mark 13:20; John 15:16).

These are the ones who join heaven and earth together through prayer for the enemies of God so that, perhaps, they will change their behaviors and confess the beautiful name of Jesus. They are the ones who emulate the humility of Jesus as expressed in Philippians chapter 2. This means the chosen of God allow God to be God while they remain servants as they were created to be. Other characteristics of the chosen are listed elsewhere in Galatians 5:22–26; Philippians 4:8; and 2 Peter 1:5–9. These are not exhaustive lists, but they point the disciple in the right direction.

LIFE AFTER PARADISE

Even though "going to heaven when we die" is not a correct biblical phrase, it remains a topic of conversation that reveals our lack of understanding. The Greek word *ouranos*, translated "heaven" in most English translations, refers to the realm or presence of God (Isaiah 66:1). The interesting point is that when Christ comes again, God's throne will be on earth (Revelation 21:2–3). But to ask a common question, though it is not a correct question, "Why does anyone want to go to heaven?" Most answer the question using terminology in Revelation 21:4, that being no more curses, no more death or suffering or sickness or pain. However, such thinking can result in the same old problem, which is self-centeredness. These, of course, are serendipities. However, should these be the primary motive for serving out Creator we then become the kind of person who the Satan falsely accused righteous Job of being. That is, we serve God for what we can get. The real issue is that we will be in the presence of God around His throne singing praises to Him, adoring Him, serving Him for all He is worth. That is the true portrait of an existence in heaven (Revelation 4).

It will be a time when heaven and earth are merged as they were intended to be in the beginning when God walked in the cool of the evening to be with His creation on earth! Hallelujah! To God be the glory! Amen!

BIBLIOGRAPHY

1. Books

Bagster, Samuel, and Sons. *The Analytical Greek Lexicon*. New York: Harper & Brothers, 1960.

Bright, John A. *History of Israel*. Philadelphia: the Westminster Press, 1976.

———. *The Kingdom of God*. Nashville: Abingdon Press, 1953.

Brueggemann, Walter. *Genesis: Interpretations: A Bible Commentary for Teaching and Preaching*. Louisville: Westminster John Knox Press, 1973.

Davis, Ellen F., and Richard B. Hays. *The Art of Reading Scripture.* Grand Rapids: Wm. B. Eerdmans Publishing, 2003.

Friberg, Barbara, and Timothy Friberg. *Analytical Greek New Testament.* Grand Rapids: Baker Book House, 1981.

Keil, C.F., and F. Delitzsch. The Pentateuch, Volume 1. Grand Rapids: Wm. B. Eerdmans Publishing, 1971.

Meyer, Ben F. *The Aims of Jesus.* Eugene: Pickwick Publications, 2002.

————. *Christus Faber.* Allison Park: Pickwick Publications, 1992.

Reicke, Bo. *The New Testament Era.* Philadelphia: Fortress Press, 1968.

Smart, James. *History and Theology in Second Isaiah*. Philadelphia: Westminster Press.

———. *The Quiet Revolution*. Philadelphia: Westminster Press, 1994.

Vine, W.E. *An Expository Dictionary of New Testament Words*. Old Tappan: Fleming H. Revell Company, 1959.

Whiston, William. *Life and Works of Flavius Josephus*. Philadelphia: the John Winston Company.

Witherington, Ben, III. *Jesus the Sage*. Minneapolis: Fortress Press, 2000.

———. *John's Wisdom*. Louisville: Westminster John Knox Press, 1995.

Wright, N.T. *Following Jesus*. Grand Rapids: William B. Eerdmans Publishing, 1994.

———. *Jesus and the Victory of God*. Minneapolis: Fortress Press, 1996.

———. *Surprised by Hope*. New York: Harper One, 2008.

———. *The Resurrection and the Son of God*. Minneapolis: Fortress Press, 2003.

2. Holy Bibles

English Standard Version (ESV). Wheaton: Good News Publishers, 2001.

King James Version, (KJV). Grand Rapids: Zondervan Publishing House, 1968.

New American Standard Bible (NASB). Anaheim: Foundation Publications, 1996.

New International Version (NIV). Colorado Springs: International Bible Society, 1983.

New Living Translation (NLT). Wheaton: Tyndale House Publishers, Inc., 1996.

The Amplified Bible Topical Reference Bible (AB). Grand Rapids: Zondervan Corporation, 1987.

Made in the USA
Middletown, DE
19 October 2023

41058033R10097